D1466576

Flexible Access Library Media Programs

FLEXIBLE ACCESS LIBRARY MEDIA PROGRAMS

Jan Buchanan

INDIANA
UNIVERSITY
NORTHWEST
LIBRARY

Z
675
.S3
B77
1991

1991
LIBRARIES UNLIMITED, INC.
Englewood, Colorado

Copyright © 1991 Libraries Unlimited, Inc.
All Rights Reserved
Printed in the United States of America

No part of this publication may be reproduced, stored in a retrieval system, or
transmitted, in any form or by any means, electronic, mechanical, photocopying,
recording, or otherwise, without the prior written permission of the publisher. An
exception is made for individual librarians and educators, who may make copies for
classroom use in a single school. Other portions of the book (up to 15 pages) may be
copied for in-service programs or other educational programs in a single school or library.
Standard citation information should appear on each page.

LIBRARIES UNLIMITED, INC.
P.O. Box 6633
Englewood, CO 80155-6633
1-800-237-6124

Library of Congress Cataloging-in-Publication Data

Buchanan, Jan.
    Flexible access library media programs / Jan Buchanan.
    xiii, 171 p. 17x25 cm.
    Includes index.
    ISBN 0-87287-834-1
    1. School libraries--Administration.   2. Media programs
(Education)   3. Libraries and students.   4. Schedules, School.
I. Title.
Z675.S3B77   1991
027.8--dc20   91-12066
                                          CIP

AKN6070

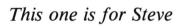

This one is for Steve

Contents

Preface

It seems as if I have spent a large portion of the waking hours of my life in a library. As a child I spent many glorious summer days at the public library in the basement of city hall and an exciting thirty minutes a week at the spacious library of my elementary school. In my secondary school years, I spent more time in the school library because I had term papers to write, or an interest in socializing, or wanted to find a book to brighten a dull weekend. My undergraduate years found me in the university library studying while my graduate years found me in some library every minute of the day and night doing research.

Asked to reflect on the various types of libraries which you have experienced during your life, I am sure your remembrances, like mine, range from school and public to corporate and academic. The specific circumstances of these encounters, of course, are as varied as the readers of this book, but there is a common element. You, the patron, had a specific need or interest which, at the time, the library could satisfy. When this need or interest arose, you could enter the library at any time during the hours of operation to have access to any resources you desired—that is, unless the library was an elementary school library. In that case you had to wait until the appointed hour of a certain day of the week to have access to the resources. How did it happen that the elementary school library came to have access limited by student age, day of the week, and hour of the day? And why does that practice still persist?

It is likely this practice occurred not because considerable thought and research by the school staff discovered a sound educational practice in limited access to the library media center, but rather it had become a habit and suited for school administrative purposes. Traditionally, library media specialists have been scheduled to meet with every class in the school once a week for a predetermined length of time. It is convenient for administrators to provide classroom teachers their contractual planning time by scheduling the library media specialist. The administrator feels comfortable in treating the library media specialist, who is paid as a teacher, as a teacher, and in knowing that each child "has library" once a week.

It is now evident through research, observation, and experience that library media programs that sufficed a decade ago are no longer viable. In the midst of the present-day information explosion, a student having just one "turn" to use the library media resources on Tuesday at 10:00 A.M. is not enough. Students must have access to information at all times, be able to think critically, integrate ideas from several sources, and use all those ideas to solve often complex problems or questions.

Information Power[1] emphasizes two program elements to meet the learning and information needs of today's school community (by providing ready access to all resources and relevant media experiences) — flexible scheduling and cooperative planning. Flexible scheduling and cooperative planning are basic to flexible access library media programs.

The successful implementation of such programs depends on the philosophy of flexible access being understood and the use of appropriate approaches and strategies. Therefore, the commitment and leadership of the library media specialist is crucial. Flexible access, however, is a school-wide program requiring the commitment and understanding of the administrators and the acceptance and support of students, staff, and parents as well. All members of the school community must assume ownership of the program. Ownership implies responsibilities. The pages of this book identify the skills and attitudes that each member must acquire to develop a successful program.

This book has been written to answer the questions that I have been asked during implementation of my flexible access library media programs and questions that have arisen as I have assisted others in developing their programs. It has been designed to assist the novice library media specialist in developing a flexible access library media program and the experienced library media specialist in gaining a new perspective on an existing program.

Those library media specialists initiating a program will want to follow the chapters in order, use appropriate forms or worksheets, and complete relevant professional activities at the end of each chapter. Those library media specialists enhancing an existing program may select chapters or parts of chapters they need. To assist the library media specialist interested in more information and more activities or in exploring research, each chapter concludes with sources for further reading.

Each of the flexible access school library media programs resulting from use of this book will be as unique as the library media specialist administering it and the school in which it thrives. It takes much time and effort to fashion a successful flexible access library media program. The more preparation initially applied to this endeavor, the more time the library media specialist will eventually have to enjoy the process and the products.

"The will to win is nothing, unless you have the will to prepare."

NOTES

[1]American Association of School Librarians and Association for Educational Communications and Technology, *Information Power: Guidelines for School Library Media Programs* (Chicago: American Library Association, 1988).

Acknowledgments

"Have you ever thought about writing a book on flexible scheduling?" a voice on the other end of the line asked. "Well ... yes, on occasion, but I need direction," I answered. "I'll be the direction," he responded. So began my acquaintance with David Loertscher, senior acquisitions editor at Libraries Unlimited. He has guided me through this sometimes all-consuming project.

My grateful appreciation to the faculties and students with whom I have worked for their cooperation, enthusiasm, and acceptance. A special thank you to my colleagues in Seminole County and Florida who have been the inspiration for my sharing ideas, trying new approaches, and constantly perfecting our program.

This book could never have materialized without the support of my family, from my parents and sister to my twin sons, Bart and Eric, each of whom assumed additional responsibilities without complaint. My deepest appreciation to my husband, Steve, who now knows more than he ever wanted to know about library media programs after painstakingly reading, responding to, and rereading the manuscript.

And a final thank you to all of the people who responded to requests to be interviewed about their experiences with flexible library media center programs. Many of these people's comments have been integrated into this manuscript and the rest provided ammunition for many of the statements in this book. The complete list of those who answered questionnaires appears in appendix H.

Chapter 1

What Is a Flexible Access Library Media Program?

This chapter provides information to assist the library media specialist in:

1. *defining flexible access library media programs and*

2. *recognizing the differences between open concept, flexibly scheduled, flexible access, and rigidly scheduled library media programs.*

If a rose is a rose is a rose, what do the words "flexible access library media program" bring to mind in educational jargon? Might the images of such a program be some of the following things happening simultaneously?

Children of varying ages are browsing for books independently.

A library media specialist is instructing a class on puppet-making.

A small group is playing a game to reinforce evaluating reference sources.

A media assistant is working with a small group of children doing research.

A child is viewing a social studies filmstrip.

These are all characteristics of a flexible access library media program, but what is new about them? you wonder. The same scenes are often evident in what have been called open concept or flexibly scheduled library media programs.

THE OPEN CONCEPT OR FLEXIBLE SCHEDULING

In past years the term *open concept* or *open library* has meant a program where students could "drop in" the media center at any time to select books or use the facilities. Too often, this concept has implied the lack of structure or a planned program. The word *open* also may imply that the library media center has previously been closed and not available to teachers and students.

1

The term *flexible scheduling* (the most popular term in the literature) has most often meant the lack of a rigid schedule. In such situations, the classroom teacher no longer brings students at 10:00 A.M. every Tuesday, leaving them smiling at the library media center door and returning thirty minutes later to retrieve them. With a flexible schedule, the teacher determines the time that library instruction is to be provided. However, the use of the word *scheduling* implies that although the administration is not determining the schedule, there is some type of routine. The schedule for library skills instruction is based on student needs and interests and is therefore different each week, but it does occur. Using this definition, teachers often prefer to schedule the same time each week even though they are theoretically not supposed to do so.

A former library media specialist once remarked as I was explaining my program,

> Oh, I used to have flexible scheduling. I put up a calendar each week for the teachers to post a time for their visits to the media center. Some of them would come to school an hour early on Monday morning to sign up for their favorite time.

Teachers wanted her to do her "curriculum" without involving them and learned how to circumvent the intended flexibility.

Beverley Fonnesbeck, of Santa Ynez, California, had a different experience with open concept. She relates:

> Spurred by curriculum reforms of the early sixties, highly cognitive and resource dependent school districts were swept by a movement to provide libraries in each elementary school. I was delighted with the opportunity to set up a library in an open concept K through six school in Anchorage, Alaska. In those early days, most librarians established their own schedules. In keeping with my philosophy, I set no schedule at all, only a blank sheet on which teachers were encouraged to write what they wanted to do in the library and when they wanted to do it. Amazingly—to me—few names were signed.
>
> Studying the teachers as I once had studied my apathetic seventh graders, I realized that the curriculum movements that brought in libraries were more foisted upon than desired by most teachers. A school library was by no means central to the teaching process in most classrooms. Until libraries were truly essential to the teaching process, they were peripheral, therefore, vulnerable. Reaching teachers with the "good news" about student involvement, flexible programming and scheduling, became my goal for the twelve years I worked in that school.[1]

RIGID SCHEDULING/FIXED SCHEDULING/SCHEDULED ACCESS

Fixed or rigid schedules as practiced in many schools consist of prescribed times for each class in the school to visit the library media center. These visits are often part of a master schedule that provides teachers with planning time. Most often, music, art, and physical education will be rotated along with library visits to achieve a predictable schedule for the teachers. Occasionally, library media specialists have input into the development of these master schedules, but more often than not, only one class is allowed in the library media center at a time and the center is available for class use only. Scheduled access programs often do not include opportunities for small groups or individuals to use the library media center for practical application of skills or for cooperative planning of lessons that integrate skills into the curriculum.

Using the library media center solely as a classroom and the library media specialist primarily as a teacher deprives students and staff of the uninhibited use of resources. Such limited use ignores the unique contribution the library media specialist can make to the educational team of the school. *Library* becomes another course in the curriculum and a laboratory that has cost the school half a million dollars to create gets tied up. Solidifying this structure even further, many library media specialists have prescribed curricula in "library science" that have been created by themselves, districts, or state departments of education. These curricula are designed to help students pass national examinations or to fill time. When the number of classes in a school building is large or the library media specialist is only part time, this schedule occupies 80 to 90 percent of the entire time the specialist is in the building. Such a schedule can appear to be a treadmill with no end in sight.

A rigid schedule ensures, however, that the library media center is filled with classes and that students are taught skills, regardless of their relevancy, and it ensures planning time for teachers. Fonnesbeck describes her experience:

> In 1979 the first teacher strike in Anchorage history focused on the issue of elementary planning time. Anxious to earn good will after the strike, the district promised time. At first the library was not involved in the trade-offs, but losses in funding made it necessary, from the district's point of view, to utilize the librarians as providers of a 30 minute per week period of release for each teacher. Needless to say, this violated every principle of my instructional philosophy; I could see no way to provide effective teaching in these circumstances. Salvaging what I could, I insisted upon keeping Fridays free to be scheduled at my discretion. With a few interested teachers, I made arrangements to give added release time if they would plan the lessons with me and relate them to the classroom. Team teaching developed with two teachers who shared my thinking about effective instruction. One teacher came regularly with her class, in exchange for a one-Friday-a-month afternoon in which I showed curriculum-related films to her students. I continued my practice of taking materials to teachers and making proposals, but the chopped-up curriculum, constant coming and going of students, and teachers' fears that they might lose their time if they gave up a minute of it for any reason made impossible the development of major learning projects or the student production that was the backbone of my instructional program. For a time I struggled to pull a rabbit out of a hat for each weekly lesson, but there weren't that many rabbits. I realized that third graders, before they were out of elementary school would have more hours of library instruction than I had in library school. That did not make sense.[2]

In 1984, Paula Montgomery questioned what had happened to the open libraries discussed in the 1960s and 1970s. Those libraries were supposed to respond to all student and teacher needs with a full range of materials and approaches. She stated that "fixed scheduling is the accepted fact in most schools."[3]

What did happen? Many administrators and library media specialists embraced the concept or the characteristics of flexible programs but lacked in-depth understanding of the program and assistance in making the program work. Often those who tried flexible scheduling, or open concept, thought it meant simply removing the existing schedule and letting "it" happen. In many instances an unprepared library media specialist tried the concept but felt considerable resistance from an uneducated staff. The results were often disastrous. Teachers were reluctant to take the initiative in scheduling media experiences and the library media specialist did not solicit participation. The library media center was unscheduled and unused. Students were no longer scheduled and no longer taught. All too often, the concept was not adapted or made workable; instead, the traditional or fixed schedule was reinstated.

FLEXIBLE ACCESS

Montgomery speculates that a combination of fixed scheduling (in which children have routine access to the library media center) and flexible scheduling (in which lessons are cooperatively planned and taught) might be the present-day *ideal* program. This type of program would provide a sense of routine and valuable instruction related to classroom activities. Florida library media specialists have termed such an arrangement a *flexible access library media program*. While such a solution may, at first glance, seem to meet the needs of two program thrusts, another view arises.

Flexible access programs are student centered. As with the whole language approach, which merges reading, writing, and literature, flexible access might be considered the *whole user* approach. Skills are taught in a systematic and sequential manner but groupings vary with the needs of the classroom curricular concept, objective, and approach. There is large-group direct instruction along with small-group and individual experiences in content areas designed by the teacher and the library media specialist together.

In February 1988, the Florida Association for Media in Education approved the following position statement:

Florida Association for Media in Education
Flexible Access Position Statement

The goal of the school library media program is to satisfy a student's natural curiosity for information, to provide opportunities for frequent learning and reading experiences, and to develop the habit of using library resources for recreation and lifelong learning. Inherent in this goal is the capacity of the program to provide teachers with opportunities to use the media center and its resources as an extension of the classroom at the time of need. Therefore, the media center program should allow flexible access to students and staff at all times, rather than operate on a schedule which preempts facilities and staff for fixed periods of time. Flexible access does not preclude an organized plan for information skills instruction, but rather allows a curriculum integrated media skills instructional program which provides relevant learning experiences for students.

Flexible access library media programs are characterized by the following criteria:

1. A media center is accessible to individuals, small groups, and classes so that students and staff may browse, explore, use, and circulate print and nonprint materials at the time of need or interest.

2. Cooperative planning by the instructional staff and the library media specialist for the use of materials and facilities in instruction.

3. Relevant information skills emanating from classroom activities, taught at the time of need or interest, and following a scope and sequence based on the curriculum needs of the school.

4. Flexible time for the library media specialist to deliver a comprehensive media program including, but not limited to, integrated information skills instruction; reference and information assistance; reading, listening and viewing motivational activities; media production; collection development and management.

In order to provide a full range of library media services and functions which an instructional program of excellence requires, the Florida Association for Media in Education (FAME) supports a flexible access library media program philosophy.[4]

How do flexible access programs differ from traditional or scheduled access programs? A flexible access program is not made by changing a few procedures in a traditional program; it is a complete change in attitude, resources, and management. It involves, among many things, a change from teaching information skills in isolation to integrating skills throughout the curriculum, a change from library media specialists working alone to cooperatively planning with teachers. Figure 1.1, prepared by the Dade County Public schools in 1988, illustrates some of the values inherent in flexible access programs.

Fig. 1.1. Elementary School Library Media Center Access Patterns.

Scheduled Access	Flexible Access
1. The use of the library media center is determined by administrative scheduling.	1. The use of the library media center is determined by teacher/student needs and interests.
2. The library media center is used for one class at a time like other classrooms in the building.	2. The library media center is used as a public facility to accommodate students of different age levels and grades simultaneously.
3. The library media center is rarely used during unscheduled periods.	3. The library media center is used all day by students involved in a variety of independent or group activities.
4. There is little correlation between classroom activities and library media center utilization.	4. Library media center visits are related to classroom activities.
5. The library media center is available for classes only.	5. The library media center is available for classes, small groups and individuals.
6. Information skills are taught in isolation.	6. Information skills lessons are determined by curriculum need.
7. Information skills are rarely reinforced in the classroom; therefore they are quickly forgotten.	7. Information skills lessons include immediate hands-on experience and reinforcement through classroom assignments.
8. Information skills instruction is confined to approximately 12 minutes per week.	8. Information skills instruction is scheduled for blocks of time determined by need.
9. There are minimal reference assignments therefore reference books are basically unused.	9. The library media center is used for reference assignments and for reference games.
10. Students have poor information retrieval skills.	10. Students learn to locate materials through frequent practice.
11. Students check out books only on assigned days.	11. Students check out books any day of the week.
12. The majority of books circulated tend to be fiction. Nonfiction circulation is minimal.	12. Students are more likely to use both fiction and nonfiction learning resources.

13. Listening, viewing, browsing, exploration and use of periodicals are minimized by time constraints.

13. Students have unrestricted opportunities to use audio-visual materials, browse, explore and use all collections.

14. Students tend to be dependent rather than independent users.

14. Students tend to use the facility independently.

15. When students reach junior high, they seldom use the library media center for recreational reading, listening, and viewing purposes.

15. When students reach junior high, they are more likely to use the library media center for recreational reading, listening, and viewing purposes.

16. The library media specialist spends the day planning and teaching.

16. The library media specialist has flexible time to promote school-wide information, reading and media motivation programs.

17. Teachers tend to view the library media center as a peripheral subject area unrelated to their own instructional assignment.

17. Teachers tend to view the library media center as an extension of their own classroom.[5]

Two other sources are valuable in defining what is meant by flexible access. Lois Kertman and Kathy Burr of Waterfront Elementary School in Buffalo, New York, describe the basic components of their flexible access program as:

- Individualized book exchange (PreK-8)
- Learning centers tied to curricular units
- Literature-based learning centers
- Computer laboratory
- Individual/small group research
- Grade projects
- Monthly enrichment activities
- Group instruction by request
- Special programs[6]

Curtis Jensen of Cedar Falls, Iowa, interviewed for this book, prefaced his remarks with the following:

> If "flexible access" means no scheduled release time for teachers, then that's the only plan I've known, and maybe I'm not the person to help with this project.
>
> If instead, "flexible access" is part of a change in philosophy, then perhaps I am involved. If "flexible access" can be part of an end to traditional library media skill lessons and a move by the library media specialist to become a more integral part of what goes on in the class-room, then I am involved. "Flexible access" is no end in itself, but is the prerequisite to resource-based teaching, to integrated media skills, and to the modern library media program.
>
> It's the first door opening.[7]

Flexible access is much more than choosing a time or allowing students to use the media center at their leisure. Flexible access affects every aspect of the library media program. It is a program pulsing with activity, adapting as necessary to make materials, personnel, and facilities readily available to the school community. A successful flexible access library media program allows students of various grade levels to participate in a variety of activities simultaneously. Large groups may use the media center in one or more sessions for curriculum-related instruction which has been planned cooperatively with the classroom teacher. Simultaneously, a small group may be doing class research, and a constant stream of individuals may be using the library media center for personal needs. The flexible access program makes each day unique. The emphasis is not on the quantity of time or instruction but on the quality. The library media specialist has time to confer with teachers; work with individual students; select, order, catalog, and process materials in addition to providing instruction and working with resource-based teaching.

The definition of this type of library media program underscorces the meaning of each term in the phrase: *flexible* and *access*. The outcome or vision of such a place brings to mind concepts such as busy, full, ever changing, needs fulfillment, center, hub, network, *heart*.

■ ═══════════════════════════════════════ ■

PROFESSIONAL ACTIVITIES

1. Use the "Elementary School Library Media Center Access Patterns" (figure 1.1) as a checklist to determine the current status of your program.

2. Make a list of the problems faced by professionals in rigidly scheduled programs then prepare a short description or scenario of your "ideal" flexible access library media program.

3. Create your own alphabet of thoughts on flexible access library media programs (refer to appendix A).

■ ═══════════════════════════════════════ ■

NOTES

[1]Beverley Fonnesbeck (library media specialist, Santa Ynez, California), response to questionnaire from author, 1990.

[2]Fonnesbeck.

[3]Paula Montgomery, "Catalyst: Open Libraries/Flexible Scheduling—Those Were the Days My Friend," *School Library Media Activities Monthly* 1 (December 1984): 44-45.

[4]"Flexible Access Position Statement," *Florida Media Quarterly* 14 (Fall 1988): 6.

[5]Dade County Public Schools, "Elementary School Library Media Centers Access Patterns," *Florida Media Quarterly* (Fall 1988): 11.

[6]Lois Kertman and Kathy Burr (library media specialists, Waterfront Elementary School, Buffalo, New York), response to questionnaire from author, 1989.

[7]Curtis Jensen (library media specialist, Cedar Falls, Iowa), response to questionnaire from author, 1990.

ADDITIONAL READINGS

Bonnell, Cathy. "Letters: For Open Communication." *School Library Journal* 34 (May 1987): 6-7.

Browne, Karen Stevens, and Linda Burton. "Timing Is Everything: Adapting to the Flexible Schedule." *School Library Journal* (December 1989): 20-23.

Gray, Gloria H. "Recipe for Enhancing Elementary School Media Centers." *Florida Media Quarterly* 14 (Fall 1988): 12-14.
    An elementary principal shares the ingredients, procedures, and results of a successful recipe for a flexible access library media program.

"A Vote for Flexible Scheduling." *Library Journal* 91 (15 September 1966): 4192-96.
    This provides a retrospective look at flexible scheduling through the survey of school librarians who implemented flexible scheduling and their responses to the experience.

Chapter 2

Why Choose a Flexible Access Library Media Program?

This chapter provides information to assist the library media specialist in:

1. *understanding the possible impact of a flexible access program on the total school curriculum,*

2. *identifying specific curriculum areas likely to be affected by a flexible access library media program, and*

3. *identifying appropriate and inappropriate reasons for selecting a flexible access library media program.*

A PERSONAL ACCOUNT

There are certain events in life etched so deeply in our minds that many years later the sounds, the smells, and the colors can be recalled. As a bride, one remembers every detail of the wedding; as a mother, each moment of the birth of a child; and for some of us, as library media specialists, the day the principal agreed to a flexible access library media program.

My principal stood leaning against the shelves in the audiovisual storage room, his arm resting next to a tape recorder, when he spoke the long-awaited words. I would like to say that he was totally convinced by my arguments, but it was actually the advent of a computer (one computer for nine hundred students and fifty staff) that precipitated this decision. The one computer would be housed in the audiovisual storage room, which could not accommodate an entire class. Each classroom teacher would be scheduled once a week to work with a few students at the computer while the others would be "right outside the door." And who was to supervise these students? Surely not the library media specialist, who was scheduled throughout the day with her own students. This seemed the opportune time to experiment with flexible scheduling.

For quite some time I had been leaving notes on the principal's desk and mentioning the advantages of flexible scheduling in every conversation. (He now refers to those days as the time his library media specialist practiced Chinese water torture disguised as flexible scheduling.) I had frequently argued that a flexible program was recommended by the state and the library profession and that "Everyone is doing it." When the principal finally agreed to pursue flexible scheduling, I soon learned that although "everyone might be doing it," no one was writing about it. To my dismay a literature search by the Public Schools Resource Center in my state revealed only a few relevant articles; attached was a note that read: "There is very little available on this topic."[1]

Prior to the principal's announcement, I had worked with every schedule imaginable as I provided planning time for teachers. In my first year at the new school my schedule included ten-minute overlaps for every class and staffing another school one day each week. We then tried an every-other-week schedule alternating with guidance, followed by eleven-week instructional blocks for intermediate grades and weekly instruction for primary students.

The final schedule consisted of cooperative planning with each teacher on Mondays, teaching of cooperatively planned lessons within a fixed schedule Tuesdays through Thursdays, and school-wide checkout on Friday. During the previous summer the books had been inventoried in June and left standing straight on the shelves. Throughout the summer the principal had guided tours through the library media center for prospective parents and other visitors and had shown with pride the neatly organized center. The first week of the new schedule had been very demanding. On Friday, as my assistant and I viewed the library media center after our nine hundred students had experienced their first checkout of the year, we decided the straightening that obviously needed doing could wait until Monday morning when we would be fresh and more able to attack what was before us.

As I entered the building Monday morning, the assistant principal met me at the door, asking that I bring a complete equipment inventory to the office. The school had been broken into over the weekend and both the district and the police needed an accurate record of the missing items. The principal soon appeared in the library media center to explain what had occurred over the weekend. There was evidence of an attempted break-in in the wing that housed the office and the library media center. The principal and the investigating officer had concluded that the library media center had been vandalized. The once-orderly books were scattered on shelves and tables, surely the work of vandals. After scrutinizing each area of the media center, I finally had to admit to the principal that nothing was amiss in the library media center. The disarray was not the deed of vandals but of his nine hundred students, who had all checked out their first books of the new school year.

Not all the schedules we designed had such disastrous results; all in fact had some positive aspects. Based on his willingness to try various scheduling, it was obvious that my principal was as eager as I to discover a "schedule" that would meet the needs of both students and staff.

Our nine hundred upper-middle-class students were fortunate to have a new library media center of forty-seven hundred square feet (approximately five to six classrooms) in size, filled with the most recent resources and staffed by one full-time media specialist, one full-time assistant, and several parent volunteers. To the casual observer the library media program at Wekiva Elementary School appeared quite adequate. The students consistently scored above grade, county, and state levels on standardized tests. Each child was instructed in the library media center following the county scope and sequence of information skills at regularly scheduled weekly intervals. However, closer scrutiny revealed that although the students were able to perform well on paper, these same students performed poorly when required to apply information skills to a problem emanating from the classroom. Many students were incapable of articulating their desires and demonstrating retrieval skills in the library media center. We felt that this inability resulted from teaching irrelevant skills in isolation and relegating them to the traditional position in the language arts curriculum.

We realized that the library media program could and should be one of the most critical elements in the instructional process. The constantly changing environment our students faced made it imperative that they acquire the necessary learning skills to cope not only with the present but also with the distant future. Although our primary goal was to develop independent media users, we wanted at the same time to motivate students through a cooperative effort of teachers and library media specialists.

Was this really flexible scheduling? Neither *flexible scheduling* nor *open concept* conveyed our intent. What we were creating was an integrated curriculum of information skills program or Totally Integrated Curriculum Through Open [Media] Center (TIC TOC), as it came to be called: a flexible access library media program that would develop independent media users through cooperative planning and a flexible schedule. With the dearth of information on the management of a flexible access program, it was necessary for us to rely on educational theory and our vision rather than on research or experience.

A LOOK AT THE RESEARCH AND EXPERT ADVICE

Impact of the Library Media Center on the Curriculum

In the decade since we began our design of a flexible access program, there have been a few studies and articles that substantiate the impact of flexible scheduling, cooperative planning, and increased services of flexible access library media programs on curriculum and learning. Elaine K. Didier documented the positive impact of school library media services on student achievement. For the purposes of her research review, *achievement* was defined as performance on tests, grade point average, and problem solving ability. Traditionally, information skills have been linked with reading, language, and writing skills; however, the research Didier reviewed shows a relationship between library media services and achievement in math, social studies, and science.[2] If one accepts that the library media program can make a positive contribution to the curriculum, then the flexible access library media program, which is designed to provide integrated information skills instruction and activities in all areas of the curriculum, is in a better position to contribute even greater benefits.

Enlarging the Impact through Integrated Information Skills

Janice R. Sly confirmed that the impact a library media program has on student learning is determined by how well the library media specialist is able to relate the functioning of the library media center to the objectives of the school through the provision of numerous and varied services. One of the specific services she cited is the correlating of skills instruction with classroom instruction through cooperatively developed activities.[3] Along the same lines, the document prepared by the U.S. Department of Education concerning research in education, *What Works*, counseled: "Students benefit academically when their teachers share ideas, cooperate in activities, and assist one another's intellectual growth."[4]

In 1984, when many professional societies were responding to concerns about the quality of education in this country, the library community gave its best advice. In *Alliance for Excellence* librarians called for teaching information skills correlated with classroom work rather than continuing the practice of isolated library lessons.[5] Research conducted by Loertscher, Ho, and Bowie on the 209 schools identified as exemplary by the U.S. Department of Education in 1986 showed that a program of library skills was only one of many components of an excellent library media program, not the main focus.[6]

In a textbook frequently used in language education courses for elementary teachers, Fox and Allen endorsed cooperative planning between the classroom teacher and the media specialist to provide materials and activities to meet instructional goals. They supported the notion that to develop into independent media users, students need opportunities to use the facilities and resources in purposeful ways. As with other learning, the learning of library skills in isolation is meaningless.[7]

Critical Thinking

In the last part of the 1980s, a great deal of discussion in the educational community centered on equipping the nation's students with better thinking skills. Mancall, Aaron, and Walker, in a concept paper written for the National Commission on Libraries and Information Science, detailed the role of the school library media program in helping students develop thinking skills. They asserted that the national attention presently directed to declining test scores, negative reports on the state of education, and the teaching of critical thinking skills makes this an opportune time for media specialists to deliver such an initiative through a curriculum-integrated information skills program. They added that one of the programming components that should be in place and adequately functioning is flexible scheduling.[8]

In an article in *School Library Media Quarterly*, Jay asserted that if educating students to think is the primary role of the school, then it is also an important role of the school library media program. Rather than considering this shift as an additional responsibility, the library media specialist should see it as a change in philosophy. As activities involving materials from the library media center are designed, thinking strategies will be incorporated. The library media specialist thus will become indispensable as an integral part of the school's critical thinking program.[9]

CURRICULAR AREAS LIKELY TO BE AFFECTED BY FLEXIBLE ACCESS

While both research and expert opinion underline the potential of the library media program to make a contribution to student achievement if that program is "integrated," the program can have an impact on a number of other, more specific, areas. The following sections provide two examples that demonstrate how the library media center program might interact with ongoing curricula.

Reading

During the 1980s, the use of basal readers as the principal method of teaching reading was questioned. Experts worried that while most young people could read at a minimal level, they neither enjoyed reading nor were achieving skills in comprehension comparable to those of children in other countries. Some schools gave teachers the option (and even encouraged them) to use literature as the basis for teaching children to read. (The California Reading Initiative was the first widespread effort.) Such shifts in individual schools opened the door to connecting reading programs and library media centers. Where teachers previously had been responsible for *teaching* children reading skills and librarians for helping young people *enjoy* reading, now both could work cooperatively to achieve both ends using the vast resources of the library media center. Suddenly, flexible access became an important tool in achieving an effective reading program. Teachers and library media specialists cooperatively could provide mounds of reading materials, story times, reading aloud, readers theatre, sustained silent reading, booktalks, reading motivational activities, and book discussions and could concentrate on the progress of both individuals and groups. At the same time, it became logical to invest half a million dollars in a well-stocked library media center and a library media specialist who could team with teachers to enhance basic literacy.

Combining the resources of the library media center, the library media specialist, and the teacher to foster literacy makes a great deal of sense in light of the experts' recommendations for structuring a reading program. *Becoming a Nation of Readers* compares the act of reading to that of playing a musical instrument. Neither is a skill mastered once and for all at a certain age, but rather something that improves through practice. The report specifies two phases of literacy.[10]

The first phase states that kindergarteners and first graders are involved in what is referred to as *emerging literacy*. For library media specialists and teachers, these are the joyful days when students learn to read the literature they have enjoyed vicariously through parents before they were old enough to attend school. Flexible access library media programs encourage the planning and delivery of frequent correlated story times and providing materials that include rich language with which students may practice these emerging skills. Research substantiates that storytelling, and reading aloud motivate children to read. When you look at children's expressions as they watch the staff dramatizing a book or poem, there is no doubt that the experiencing of good literature stimulates the desire to learn to read. When the teacher and the library media specialist collaborate to create the best possible experiences for these budding readers, it is not surprising that an extremely high rate of success is achieved. In fact, the potential for success when using the tool of flexible access is so high that reverting to a rigid schedule is unthinkable.

The second phase suggested in the report also has implications for flexible access library media programs. This phase is known as *extending literacy*. After children learn the rudiments of reading skill and reading enjoyment, they are equipped to explore literature and nonfiction in depth. Thus, in higher grades, teachers and library media specialists help students explore every type of genre and information source while building comprehension skills, enjoyment, and breadth of knowledge. Regardless of the skill of each child, the library media program provides those opportunities to practice and the materials which will broaden both interests and educational depth.

To achieve true literacy, both the teacher and the library media specialist must believe the statement in *What Works*: "Children improve their reading ability by reading a lot. Reading achievement is directly related to the amount of reading children do in school and outside."[11] But more than just belief is at work in flexible access programs. These programs provide activities that promote individual reading and make books easily available to children. Everywhere a child looks there are attractive books begging to be read: in their desks, in their rooms, and in the library media center. As children are encouraged through reading incentive programs to read more, they develop a better attitude about reading and make greater gains in reading comprehension.

A number of reading experts raised a red flag when they discovered that in "basalized" reading programs students spent more time filling in skill sheets than actually reading. These persons concluded that if we value reading, books will be incorporated into our reading programs. However, this common sense approach often is not applied in practice because teachers are preparing students for national examinations. They know that concentration on skills exercises will produce results, while just allowing students to read seems risky. How can we know that students will all be exposed to the same skills and be able to pass the test if we just let them read? Library media specialists can help teachers make this leap of faith, using the flexibility of their programs and the mountains of reading materials at their disposal. Research supports both logic and faith, since children who read widely also score high on national examinations.

As evidence that library media specialists have always been on the right track, Loertscher, Ho, and Bowie found that a major component of library media programs in exemplary elementary schools is their emphasis on promoting reading. In the 1960s, when every elementary school received substantial funds from the federal government to buy books, most schools created libraries rather than classroom collections of books. When library media specialists were hired to create and maintain these collections, these people established programs to see that the newly purchased materials were used. Reading stories aloud, storytelling, and reading motivation activities were the bread and butter of library media center programs. The challenge of the 1980s has been to merge these efforts into the total reading program.

Whole Language

Almost simultaneously with the directive to teach reading using literature, the whole language movement became popular. Whole language is an integrated approach to speaking, writing, listening, and reading. Integrated language views the curriculum as a whole rather than as isolated subjects or units and encourages high levels of participation in meaningful activities. This holistic approach uses a wide variety of literature: trade books, poems, magazines, and literary anthologies in conjunction with, in addition to, or in lieu of basal readers. Thus the concept of whole language is broader than literature-based reading instruction. Just as with literature-based reading, the flexible access program of the library media center is a perfect tool to foster whole language. In addition to storytelling and reading aloud, library media center resources can be used as a basis for dramatics, puppetry, video production, book discussions, readers theatre, oral expression, book writing, illustrating, and the information skills instruction needed for all of these. Veatch's description of the ingredients of whole language places library media services at the heart of any successful program: self-selection, pupil-choice, and a wide range of resources from which to choose.[12]

STUDENT BENEFITS

Why did this author choose a flexible access library media program? The program supports and enhances all areas of the curriculum and utilizes the facilities and materials. But most important, it employs the unique opportunity a library media specialist has to develop a love of learning in each student.

The retention of facts is secondary to the knowledge of strategies for learning and skill in information retrieval. If we are committed to teaching individual students rather than teaching subjects, we have no choice but to select a flexible access library media program. Such programs increase individual attention to students, promote active participation of the child in learning by doing, and provide alternative methods for learning. Although skills as identified by the state or county curricula are incorporated in the program, emphasis is on students' attitude as well as their intellect. Each endeavor continues to reinforce the student's ability to gather, evaluate, and use all available resources. A flexible access program focuses on providing creative opportunities for students to discover new interests, compare ideas, and make decisions as they acquire the skills for independent, lifelong media use. A flexible access program provides the daily opportunity to "practice what I preach," be it through art, social studies, reading, or math: relevant teaching and retained learning. My reason for choosing a flexible access library media program is most aptly conveyed by these well-known axioms, which have graced my office since my first year as a media specialist:

Give a man a fish and he will eat for a day.
Teach him how to fish and he will eat for a lifetime.

Tell me, I forget.
Show me, I remember.
Involve me, I understand.

A flexible access program should not be chosen simply for reasons of time flexibility. Often when elementary library media specialists gather, the conversation turns to scheduling. I have frequently heard my colleagues lament how busy they are. The majority of their day is consumed with instruction, leaving only a few minutes for a hurried lunch and little time for materials selection, processing, maintenance, or the myriad other professional responsibilities. The next utterance is usually: "I wish I had flexible access like you and then I would have time to get everything done." Granted, the removal of the weekly regime of classes does allow more time for program responsibilities other than instruction. However, this should never be the reason for implementation of a flexible access program. The focus of a library media program must be on the patrons it serves. I can state unequivocally that a flexible access library media program is not easier, but it certainly is better.

DIFFERENT SETTINGS, DIFFERENT EFFECTS

As I have seen the flexible program evolve, I have observed the following signs of its effectiveness:

- the increased participation of students, staff, and community in the cooperatively planned media program;

- the quality and creativity of student-produced media related work;

- a rise in standardized test scores;

- the transfer of learning to public library and middle school media centers as a result of "real library" experiences; and

- the positive attitudes of all involved in the program. With skilled, independent media users, the media staff is better able to use time and therefore provide the full range of services a school library media program of excellence requires.

What program wouldn't succeed serving upper-middle-class students with adequate staffing, modern facilities, and abundant resources? That is the question I was often asked when presenting Wekiva's TIC TOC program to my colleagues. Obviously the staffing, facilities, and resources enhanced the program, but I was convinced that the program could be successful anywhere, or as I often said, "even in a closet."

In 1986, I found the perfect library media center in which to test my theory. Wilson Elementary School was everything that Wekiva Elementary School was not. Wilson's 360 students had a media center of eighteen hundred square feet, a part-time media specialist, a part-time assistant, and no parent volunteers. It had minimal, outdated resources. Not only did the room, originally built as an auditorium in 1928, accommodate the simultaneous activities of a flexible access program, but it also housed a clinic (behind the curtains on the stage), the speech pathologist's office, and the music classroom two days a week. Our experiences in developing a flexible access library media program tailormade for Wilson Elementary School confirmed that such a program can be successful anywhere. Flexible access can be the program of choice, regardless of the facilities, materials, enrollment, or size of the staff.

If you wait to begin a program until all conditions are ideal, the time will never arrive. The facilities will always need improving, additional help will always be needed, or the collection will need developing. The condition that must be met is to have a library media specialist totally committed to the flexible access concept and willing to work harder than ever before. As George Bernard Shaw said: "People who get on in this world are the people who get up, look for the circumstances they want, and if they can't find them, make them." (*Mrs. Warren's Profession*, 1893).

PROFESSIONAL ACTIVITIES

1. Consult the bibliography for further readings. Record reasons cited for implementing a flexible access library media program.

2. Locate successful flexible access library media programs. Ask the media specialists why these programs were started.

3. Prepare a written rationale for flexible access implementation in your school.

4. Determine your school's educational philosophy. List suggestions for putting the philosophy "in action" through a flexible access library media program.

NOTES

[1]George Plumleigh, Dorothy Baird, Mary Baker, and Luella Sprague, "Los Alamitos: The School Library Media Program of 1977," *School Library Journal* 24 (October 1977): 74-79; Johanna Wood, "Media Programs in Open Space Schools," *School Media Quarterly* (Spring 1976): 207.

[2]Elaine K. Didier, "An Overview of Research on the Impact of School Library Media Programs on Student Achievement," *School Library Media Quarterly* 14 (Fall 1985): 33-36, ERIC Journal 330 166; Elaine K. Didier, "Research on the Impact of School Library Media Programs on Student Achievement — Implications for School Media Professionals," in *School Library Media Annual*, ed. Shirley L. Aaron and Pat Scales (Englewood, Colo.: Libraries Unlimited, 1984), 2: 343-53.

[3]Janice R. Sly, *Domains: Knowledge Base of the Florida Performance Measurement System, Domain 9.0: Library Media Services* (Tallahassee, Fla.: Florida Department of Education, 1985).

[4]United States Department of Education, *What Works: Research about Teaching and Learning* (Washington, D.C.: U.S. Government Printing Office, 1986), 67.

[5]United States Department of Education, *Alliance for Excellence: Librarians Respond to a Nation at Risk* (Washington, D.C.: U.S. Government Printing Office, 1984).

[6]David V. Loertscher, May Lein Ho, and Melvin M. Bowie, "Exemplary Elementary Schools and Their Library Media Centers: A Research Report," *School Library Media Quarterly* (Spring 1987): 147-53.

[7]Sharon E. Fox, and Virginia Garibaldi Allen, *The Language Arts: An Integrated Approach* (New York: Holt, Rinehart and Winston, 1983).

[8]Jacqueline C. Mancall, Shirley L. Aaron, and Sue A. Walker, "Educating Students to Think: The Role of the School Library Media Program: A Concept Paper Written for the National Commission on Libraries and Information Science," *School Library Media Quarterly* 15 (Fall 1986): 18-27.

[9]M. Ellen Jay, "The Elementary School Library Media Teacher's Role in Educating Students to Think: Suggested Activities for Fostering the Development of Thinking Skills," *School Library Media Quarterly* 15 (Fall 1986): 28-32.

[10]R. C. Anderson, E. H. Hiebert, J. A. Scott, and I. A. G. Wilkerson, *Becoming a Nation of Readers: The Report of the Commission on Reading* (Washington, D.C.: U.S. Department of Education, 1985).

[11]United States Department of Education, *What Works* (Washington, D.C.: U.S. Department of Education, 1987), 8.

[12]Jeannette Veatch, "En Garde, Whole Language," in *School Library Media Annual*, ed. Jane Bandy Smith (Englewood, Colo.: Libraries Unlimited, 1988), 6: 8-14.

ADDITIONAL READINGS

Aaron, Shirley L. "The Role of Basic Information Skills in an Educational Program of Excellence." *School Library Media Activities Monthly* 1 (December 1984): 27-30.

Barron, Daniel D. "Institutionalizing School Library Media Programs." *School Library Media Activities Monthly* 6 (February 1990): 48-50.

Berkowitz, Bob, and Joyce Berkowitz. "Thinking Is Critical: Moving Students beyond Location." *School Library Media Activities Monthly* 3 (May 1987): 25-27, 50.

Brown, David M. "A Half-Time Compromise to the Whole Language Approach." In *School Library Media Annual*, edited by Jane Bandy Smith, 6: 36-42. Englewood, Colo.: Libraries Unlimited, 1988.

Costa, Arthur L. *Developing Minds, a Resource Book for Teaching Thinking*. Alexandria, Va.: Association for Supervision and Curriculum Development, 1985.
Costa provides numerous strategies, activities, and resource lists for developing a critical thinking curriculum, many of which are of particular interest to library media specialists.

Duff, Ann. "Who Cares If There's an Open Schedule?" *Florida Media Quarterly* 14 (1988): 7.
In an open letter to an elementary principal, a district media supervisor describes what flexible access can do to revitalize the media program.

Haycock, Ken. "Whole Language Issues and Implications." In *School Library Media Annual*, edited by Jane Bandy Smith, 6: 15-19. Englewood, Colo.: Libraries Unlimited, 1988.
Haycock discusses the implications of whole language programs for publishers, teachers, and library media specialists.

Jachymn, Nora K., Richard L. Allington, and Kathleen A. Broikou. "Estimating the Cost of Seatwork." *The Reading Teacher* 43 (October 1989): 30-34.

Loertscher, David V. "On Joining the Unhooked Generation; or How and Why to Junk the Scheduling Habit." *Hoosier School Libraries* 14 (October 1974): 17-20.

Magers, Jody L. "Advantages of Using a Flexible Open Schedule in Elementary School Libraries." *Ohio Media Spectrum* 38 (Fall 1986): 42.

Markuson, Carolyn. "Readers' Queries." *School Library Media Quarterly* 16 (Winter 1988): 133-34.

Markuson's response highlights the library media program areas and issues that become lost with a fixed schedule. An excellent resource for developing arguments for a flexible access program and for suggestions for coping with a fixed schedule.

Stahlschmidt, Agnes. "Support for the Whole Language Program—What the Library Media Specialist Can Do." *School Library Media Activities Monthly* 6 (December 1989): 31.

As the title implies, the author lists specific contributions the library media specialist can make to the school's whole language program.

Wilkens, Lea-Ruth C. *Supporting K-5 Reading Instruction in the School Library Media Center*. Chicago: American Library Association, 1984.

The author considers the library media specialist the "special ingredient" in the school's reading program and provides suggestions for how the media specialist can contribute to the program.

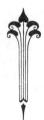# Chapter 3

Designing a Flexible Access Library Media Program

This chapter provides information to assist the library media specialist in:

1. *assessing the need for change to a flexible access library media program.*

2. *identifying areas which must be considered prior to implementation of a flexible access library media program.*

3. *designing a unique flexible access library media program.*

PREPARING TO DESIGN A PROGRAM

The concept of flexible access permeates every aspect of the school's educational program. The difference between a good and an excellent flexible access library media program is organization and preparation. Program development follows a logical sequence:

1. Evaluate your own attributes.

2. Conduct a needs assessment.

3. Convince the principal.

4. Deal with administrative concerns.

5. Involve the teachers.

6. Involve a library media advisory committee.

While it is important to follow a logical strategy, it is more important to know when to put all that aside: to bend a rule, to change a policy, to try a new procedure, to be spontaneous. On many occasions I have remarked to my principal that I have been so flexible that day that "I'm bent out of shape."

In the initial years of the flexible access program my library media clerk used to reprimand me for "not being strict enough with the teachers" by not making them follow established procedures to the letter. Consider the policies, procedures, and suggestions to be written in pencil, not set in stone, because they are useful only if they, as well as the library media specialist, are flexible.

Library Media Specialist Attributes

Although each flexible access program is inherently unique, there is a common element in every successful program: the total commitment of the library media specialist and the principal. It is not sufficient to be dedicated to the concept of flexible access library media programs; both the library media specialist and the principal must also be dedicated to the delivery of such programs. Although all participants should assume ownership, the library media specialist must provide the leadership. I once heard leadership defined as making what you believe in happen. The library media specialist must accept the responsibility of conveying that belief to the school community by being a continual presence throughout the school. Research has shown that central to the success and efficiency of any library media program is the person who administers the services.

Successful flexible access programs require a tremendous amount of time and energy. The library media specialist must be willing not only to take the risk of leaving the secure and familiar routine of regularly scheduled classes, but also to devote countless hours to the preparation, implementation, evaluation, and continual adaptation of the program. Therefore, it is imperative that the library media specialist be convinced that a flexible access library media program is the best program to deliver and become proactive rather than reactive. The program does not mold the library media specialist, rather, the library media specialist shapes the program. Those characteristics and attitudes not present in a fixed access program will not be present in a flexible access program.

Program knowledge is acquired through continual education. Professional education may take the form of reading broadly and interacting with colleagues. Participation in professional activities such as workshops or conferences provides valuable opportunities for learning. The specialized skills one needs for a successful flexible access library media program can also be gained by emulating mentors or role models. As skills and knowledge are obtained they must be communicated to the school community and time needs to be allotted to train others to become flexible access leaders.

The library media specialist must have a positive attitude. The library media specialist is there to serve students and staff and must always be aware of the attitudes and behaviors encouraging or impeding access. Flexible access programs demand tolerance, patience, a high frustration threshold, and a sense of humor. Program preparation and organization encourage but do not ensure student and staff participation, but a smile and flexibility do. As we implement change we must exemplify the trait we want our students, staff, and community to have: flexibility.

Needs Assessment

Chapter 2 emphasized the need for a flexible access library media program as a central component of the educational program. This need for a flexible access program must be established not only through theory and logic, but also through patron surveys, media staff surveys, user activity, and in-house observation. Figure 3.1 provides a sample questionnaire from which appropriate questions might be extracted and to which others might be added. It asks teachers to estimate how much they would use a flexible access program if one were available. The problem, however, is that one is asking a teacher who may not *know* if a pattern of service might be superior. Those totally satisfied with the current situation and who have not experienced anything else are not likely to give visionary responses. It is those who are somewhat troubled by the current service who will be sympathetic to change. An example of how hard it is to ask visionary responses from persons who are satisfied with the status quo is people's reaction to the invention of the airplane. In the early days of flight, skeptics denied that the airplane would ever become a form of mass transportation — they could not envision the idea. Indeed, many felt that it was unnatural for human beings to fly. Time has shown the shortsightedness of their vision, but it has shown, as well, the inexorable movement of progress — and the realization of the visions of a few.

Prior to the implementation of our flexible access program, fourth-grade teachers made these comments on their needs assessment forms: "We would like more media experiences coordinated with in-school leveling" and "We want continuous skills rather than one large skill unit. Our students need review each week." Second-grade teachers requested "small group checkout." Fifth-grade teachers stated the need thus: "Each grade should be involved from the very beginning in the inception, approval and implementation of all media schedules that involve that grade." Our specific learning disabilities teacher indicated: "Scheduling should be more flexible." All of these comments and suggestions indicated to us that the time was right for a flexible access library media program. Not only did the data collected from the evaluation assist in effecting change, but we also used that information to design relevant teacher education activities and many of the individual program components.

Convincing the Principal

The principal who agrees to the implementation of a flexible access program must make a commitment of support and energy. The committed principal is aware that the process of developing a successful program is gradual and that knowing the benefits of the program and being able to explain them to the staff and community is paramount. The administrator assumes the role of advocate along with the library media specialist.

It is a rare occurrence for the principal to request a flexible access library media program. In most instances the library media specialist initiates the concept and not only must define flexible access but also must convince the principal of the benefits of such a program and provide suggestions for implementation.

Fig. 3.1. Library Media Center Needs Assessment Questionnaire.

Date _____

LIBRARY MEDIA CENTER NEEDS ASSESSMENT QUESTIONNAIRE

Respond to the questions as follows:

Y for yes   N for no   X for not applicable

1. Other than your regularly scheduled library visit, are there times in your week when you would like to use the library media center as follows:

_____ individuals sent from your classroom at any time?

_____ small groups sent from your classroom at any time?

_____ small groups sent from your classroom by appointment?

_____ scheduled class visits for instruction?

_____ scheduled class visits for circulation?

_____ class use upon request?

2. Would you prefer to consult with the library media specialist for instructional planning as:

_____ an individual teacher?

_____ part of a team, department, or grade level?

_____ a member of a curriculum committee?

_____ not at all

3. In planning for instruction with your library media specialist, would you:

_____ have a regularly scheduled planning time?

_____ make appointments for planning sessions as needed?

_____ complete planning sheets, if requested, prior to planning?

_____ assist in the selection and evaluation of materials?

_____ involve the library media specialist in instructional activities using library media materials/technology?

_____ have difficulty in scheduling the library media center for the lessons or units planned?

_____ participate in the evaluation of library media center-based lessons or units?

_____ inform the library media specialist of assignments that call for use of media resources?

_____ none of the above

4. If access to the library media center were not an issue, how do you think you would use those facilities and resources in your teaching?

The most accurate definition of a flexible access library media program is the one formed in each individual school. Each principal has a vision or mission for the school, which is reflected in the philosophy of education shared by the staff and the community. The flexible access program enhances and extends that vision. The library media specialist can assist the school in creating its definition by developing a program outline describing, in terms of the shared vision, what can be done with a flexible access library media program compared to what is presently being done with a limited access program. The outline definition might detail one area or include numerous examples.

The school's philosophy is the basis for the flexible access library media program created at Bennett Park Montessori Center in Buffalo, New York. As library media specialist Kathy Kren states:

> Originally, the school had a few meager resources in the library but wanted some form of open program to match the Montessori philosophy. The fourth year of operation, the present library media specialist was hired. During the interview, both the principal and the library media specialist agreed that a flexible access program would be initiated. Because of the Montessori philosophy, teachers wanted their students to be able to do many research-oriented but student-selected projects.[1]

The flexible access program is defined as consisting of three major activities as outgrowths of the Montessori philosophy:

1. *Student research*. Individuals and small groups stream into the center all day doing research and independent projects which they have selected themselves. These groups are assisted by the specialist, another adult, or older student. Students are expected to do much self-directed research.

2. *Student enjoyment*. Individuals and small groups come at any time during the day to find and check out materials for personal use. There is a lot of sharing of popular materials among students. Browsing for five minutes or forty-five minutes is valued activity. The Montessori philosophy requires that the students have a purpose at all times within a wide latitude of choice.

3. *Units of instruction*. Teachers wanting to do lengthy or in-depth topical studies plan with the library media specialist in advance for activities and appropriate materials. Joint planning takes place to insure that materials are available in the center or by interlibrary loan, that appropriate activities are designed to take advantage of the materials, and that any library skills needed to use the materials are planned. The planning for these resource-based teaching units is done at grade level lunches or during the teacher's planning time. If the library media specialist is not free, the administration will provide a person (sometimes themselves) to cover in the library media center while the planning takes place.[2]

Whether the focus for defining your flexible access library media program is singular or varied, concentrate on activities that support areas or projects the principal has identified as important. Is the use of technology in the classroom a primary focus? Include in the definition ideas for enhancing use of technology through the media program. The school's curricular emphasis also can be extended through flexible access. If creative writing or daily oral language are curriculum priorities, suggest means for extending classroom learning through the media program. Describe the role a flexible access program can play in the school's drop-out prevention or at-risk program. Examples of the role of a flexible access library media program at each grade level in several diverse areas of the curriculum would also be effective in forming the individual school's definition.

Marlene Lazzara describes her experience at Henking Elementary School (K-3) in Glenview, Illinois, a National Council of Teachers of English Center for Excellence, 1987-1989 as follows:

> Learning Centers at the time I came to the district were very traditional, i.e., classes came in at half-hour periods once a week for story hours and/or library skills. Also, the primary classroom teachers sent reading groups down daily. There was very little connection between activities in the library media center and what was happening in the classrooms. Classroom teachers used this half-hour as planning time and rarely communicated with the library media staff about their students' needs.
>
> As I began to look at the research on learning styles and effective schools, it became clear that we needed to change our program to better serve our population. I realized learning does not take place in a vacuum. We have a very full curriculum and I wasn't comfortable with the idea that there were no connections in the library media program. As the library media specialist, it is my responsibility to create opportunities for all students to use the Learning Center to extend and enhance the learning taking place in the classroom. With the traditional schedule, this wasn't happening.
>
> So we did away with the traditional one-half hour per week for storytime or library skills and adopted a flexible schedule planned by classroom teachers and me to provide meaningful activities for students. This was not an easy transition. What actually happened is that both my principal and I supported the concept and our staff, while supporting it in principle, did not share our enthusiasm when we told them they could no longer send reading groups to the library media.
>
> Although the transition hasn't always been smooth, we've used a flexible schedule since 1984. All activities in the library media center are jointly planned by me and the classroom teachers. These plans take many forms. Since our kindergarten through third grade school has a focus on beginning and emerging readers, the Learning Center program emphasizes the language arts.[3]

A needs assessment, surveys, and interviews can provide the impetus for convincing the administration of the need for a flexible access program.

Nell Brown of Palm Coast, Florida, relates her experiences with a principal and teaching staff:

> I was a complaining teacher and one day the principal said to me, "You will be the librarian tomorrow. Put your money where your mouth is." I walked into a rigid schedule, six classes a day, five days a week. There was no time to do anything but meet classes. I knew from experience that talking about it would not work.
>
> I did a survey of services wanted that we could not provide. I did counts of students we had to turn away. Since I had a clerk, we started to provide access on top of the rigid schedule. We also interviewed teachers and talked about their needs of sending students at times other than scheduled times. We also had our representative to the classroom teachers association investigate whether our current jobs were violating the master contract. (Were we teaching too many students with no planning time?)
>
> After having juggled both types of schedules, we told the teachers that we could not continue doing both types of activities. The teachers then requested that the situation be looked at. The administration decided to provide additional teachers to replace the teacher contractual time missed by not coming to the LMC on a weekly basis. While that was great news, we did not immediately jump on the flexible access bandwagon. We spent time planning with the teachers how to build the new program. We did PR with the school community to let the parents know what changes would be taking place and the benefits of those changes.
>
> When we finally opened as a flexible access program, the faculty became our strongest supporters along with our administrator.[4]

The county, district, or state curriculum offers opportunities to show how flexible access can improve instruction. If a new science curriculum has been introduced, cite examples of experiences that will broaden the curriculum and provide a bibliography of related resources available in the media center. Offer curriculum correlations that emphasize cooperative planning and the integration of skills. If the basal reading program introduces folktales at the third-grade level, describe possible activities and the role the classroom teacher and the library media specialist play in them. Jo Ann Gadicke of Cheboygan, Wisconsin, was successful in using such an approach with her principal:

> Last spring our district chose a new reading series that was not "whole language experienced based" but they were going to use the whole language approach. I knew teachers would be needing more resources from the library, so I approached my principal with the idea of flexible scheduling to allow me to pursue resource based teaching. He asked me to present my ideas to our school effectiveness team for their input. My suggestion was to have the children do a book exchange of fifteen minutes three times a month, with a half an hour library period once a month at which time I would do an author appreciation. I also wanted to work with the fourth and fifth graders once a month for at least an hour on a library skill rather than having

fifteen minutes each week. The effectiveness team was divided, but there were some strong supporters of the idea. I was asked to present my ideas to the whole faculty on the last day of school in June. I had succeeded in having our media center open for portions of the summer school schedules and had worked out a media curricula chart for summer school teachers to use. They seemed responsive to that, so I added more portions to the chart for this school year. I used the chart to try to show teachers some of the possibilities of what we could do with more flexible scheduling and integrating library skills in curricular areas. The majority of the staff were willing to give resource based teaching and flexible scheduling a try.[5]

The unique definition of the flexible access library media program might be derived from the school's comprehensive plan. If increasing test scores is a high priority, incorporate appropriate ideas in the definition shared with the principal. A tailormade definition fosters understanding but by no means ensures acquiescence.

One of the simplest means of providing principals with convincing arguments for flexible access is through conversation. Opportunities to elucidate the benefits of the program often arise during a principal's impromptu visit to the media center or even a chance meeting in the staff lounge. The creative library media specialist can use any occasion to promote flexible access library media programs.

Articles written by administrators or teachers that document the merits of flexible access have often influenced a reluctant principal. Leaving a folder of selected reprints and a note on the principal's desk offering to discuss anything of interest is a subtle but effective technique. Visiting successful programs can inspire administrators to consider developing a unique program of their own.

Administrative Concerns

Like library media specialists, even principals who are committed to a flexible access library media program have some apprehension about implementing a program for which they have had no training. Principals often fear that without regularly scheduled classes the library media specialist will not be busy with students all day and will act more like a public librarian. How can the principal justify staffing the library media center with certified personnel who are paid as teachers if they are not going to teach as teachers? The principal should be aware that although one of the roles of the library media specialist is teacher, the specialist is not primarily a teacher and has unique contributions to make to the school. Library media specialists in programs where circulation and instruction are provided in forty-minute periods for all classes each week have only a few hours left for their other roles and responsibilities. Itemizing the activities carried on by the library media specialist during a typical day can help alleviate the principal's anxiety. After flexible access program initiation, weekly or monthly summaries can be submitted to the principal.

Of foremost concern to the principal is how contractual planning time can be provided for teachers. Classroom teacher contracts mandate a specified amount of planning or break time, and although principals are aware that it is not educationally sound to provide this time by using the library media specialist, they often have not explored other scheduling possibilities. The library media specialist can suggest options that have been successful in other schools or design a site-specific plan. Planning time for the classroom teacher might be provided by:

1. Designing a rotation schedule for special area teachers. For example, each student would receive instruction in physical education three days per week and in music and art one day per week.

2. Employing substitutes or using instructional aides to supervise classes. Activities could be scheduled that require a minimum of preparation but a maximum of benefit, such as sustained silent reading in the intermediate grades or reading aloud in the primary grades.

3. Satisfying specified planning time on a weekly rather than a daily basis.

The principal will be concerned about the library media staffing requirements for such a program. The staffing of the library media center should allow for the library media specialist to conduct planning time with teachers and to plan and prepare for activities. The use of adult library media assistants for duties outside the media center, such as bus duty or cafeteria duty, is discouraged. Library media personnel should be provided at a level that allows uninterrupted access to library media center facilities, resources, and personnel for students and staff throughout the day.

Students participating in a flexible access library media program do not "have library" once a week. This concept is difficult to convey, and the principal who has the responsibility of communicating the program to the parents, community, and school board has reason to be anxious. Supply the principal with a list of benefits from the administrator's perspective. Emphasize that flexible access library media programs ensure the best use of expensive resources, customize teaching and learning, and build staff morale. As with the library media specialist, the more knowledge of and experience with the program a principal has, the more vigorous a proponent that principal will become.

Involving the Teachers

A library media specialist initiating a flexible access library media program must possess the ability to initiate and sustain communication with groups and individuals. My principal and I agreed when he was first entertaining the thought of a "flexible schedule" that I would survey each grade level's team of teachers. At each regularly scheduled planning session, after discussing the activities that would be occurring in the media center, I delicately queried each group as to their feelings about our implementing a flexible schedule. The reactions ranged from uninterested to hostile. One of the intermediate teams informed me: "We have discussed what you do in the media center and it has no bearing on what we do in the classroom." I regained my composure and gave them my best textbook response, that what I did indeed *did* have a bearing on what they did in the classroom and that I would like an opportunity to show them how. I certainly displayed much more confidence than I felt, but unless I appeared in total control, what teacher would be willing to give me the opportunity to prove that such a program would work?

More often than not the concept of flexible access library media programs is not a popular one with classroom teachers. The library media specialist must be able to understand both the personal and the professional frame of reference of these teachers. Teachers who are unfamiliar with the program resent what they consider to be the loss of their planning or break time, which was once afforded by the library media specialist. They are sometimes bitter that they have a role in this new program and that "library time" no longer means dropping their students off at the door to the media center. During the year prior to full implementation of the program, as I was attempting to schedule a planning time with one of the teachers, I realized that this approach certainly was not going to be easy. She remarked: "The library media specialist at my other school knew what to teach. We didn't have to plan."

Get teachers involved in the flexible access program—include them in the decision-making process to ensure that services respond to their needs, preferences, and priorities. This reinforces that they are receiving rather than losing. To get them into your camp, try the following:

1. Compile a list of possible services.

2. Survey staff. Ask staff to prioritize the list and offer suggestions for additional services. The survey will not only determine their understanding of existing services but will also make them aware of potential services.

3. Compile data and determine what services may best support flexible access program goals and objectives.

4. Inform staff. Initially this might be done through displays and announcements. The appropriate explanation of services and the procedure for obtaining each service are included in the teacher handbooks. Figure 3.2 is a portion of such a sheet.

5. Evaluate and adapt. The evaluation process is continual and provides modifications of the services offered based on teacher needs, preferences and priorities and the program goals and objectives.

When I happen to see the television commercial that advises "Never let them see you sweat," I am reminded not only of that experience with a teacher who didn't want to plan but of many other experiences I have had with flexible access library media programs. The staff will be uncomfortable with the concept; often the administration and even the parents may be apprehensive. The library media specialist must be enthusiastic and give the impression of being in control and knowing the direction in which the program is headed. When we, as library media specialists, know where we want to go, others will likely follow if the leadership we provide is based on knowledge and expertise.

Fig. 3.2. Services of Plainview Elementary Library Media Center.

Curriculum Integration

The library media specialist provides appropriate materials in a variety of formats to help all kinds of learners. The library media specialist assists in planning appropriate activities and materials for teaching content, enrichment, or reinforcement. Bibliographies of all media resources may be generated on any subject and in any format. Requests indicated on the Planning Sheet.

Literature Appreciation Experiences

All media program activities are literature-based and designed to promote the enjoyment of reading. In addition the media program provides opportunities for oral reading, storytimes, or booktalks and provides displays, exhibits, and reading lists.

Information Skills Instruction

Large group, small group, or individual instruction for specific media-related skills is provided by the library media specialist at the time of need or interest. Skills are taught according to the county scope and sequence of information skills and are integrated into all areas of the curriculum. Times for skills instruction are arranged during regularly scheduled planning sessions.

Information Skills Application

Activities are provided for large group, small group, and individual application of information skills. These experiences are cooperatively planned during regularly scheduled planning sessions.

Media Production

Instruction and assistance in the production of instructional materials is provided by the media staff. Instruction for student produced media such as transparencies, slides, videotapes, and computer programs may also be scheduled.

Professional Development

In-service opportunities are offered periodically in the areas of technology, children's literature, information sources, and new materials. Equipment operation training may be scheduled as necessary. The Professional Library houses books, periodicals and other materials of professional interest. Newly acquired print and nonprint materials are displayed in the Professional Library prior to being placed in circulation. Individual items of interest are routed by means of an Article Alert.

Issues for the Library Media Center Advisory Committee

There is nothing more frustrating than trying to instill major change by oneself. While leadership of the program rests with the library media specialist, the help of a library media advisory committee can be invaluable. Such a committee is suggested in many national documents and articles. It should be a small group of influential persons who can not only create policy but also rethink programs. The committee should consist of the library media specialist, the principal, teachers, parents, and students (as appropriate). This committee helps decide the degree and numbers of needs, where the program will go, the activities likely to achieve the goals, the objectives, and how the library media center program will be evaluated. Whether or not a formal committee is organized, each of the following issues must be addressed, for teachers who feel that a program is being imposed from above may find it difficult to accept. True, there are instances when a heavy hand is necessary, but change is usually much more palatable if those who are affected help shape that change.

DESIGNING THE PROGRAM

Many groups need to be involved as a flexible access program is in the developmental stage. A library media specialist in concert with the school administration and staff should design the actual program progress in a logical fashion. Four main steps of program design are outlined here: goals, objectives, priorities, and policies and procedures.

Goals

The first task in designing a flexible access library media program is the development of written goals. The goals of the library media program are the long-range desired outcomes. All objectives, strategies and activities relate to the media program goals. Flexible access library media program goals should be all encompassing, philosophically appropriate, and clearly stated. Goals, unlike objectives, cannot be measured. Goals direct the program and should be articulated to the students and staff. Preparing one concise sentence or phrase as the goals statement will ensure that your patrons (and you) will never be in doubt about what you are trying to do. My flexible access library media program has one goal: "To develop independent library media users." This goal encompasses all patrons and extends over an indefinite period of time.

Objectives

Once the flexible access library media program goals are established, determine the library media program objectives. The objectives are the quantifiable components of the goals and should be specific, attainable, and measurable. The objectives of a flexible access program essentially indicate what will be done. Three such objectives for developing independent media users might be to:

1. Provide daily opportunities for students to browse, explore, and use all resources of the library media center.

2. Provide teachers with opportunities to create library media center-based units of instruction at least on a monthly basis.

3. Provide assistance to students in carrying out resource-based learning assignments and activities each time those activities happen.

Priorities

The library media specialist and the library advisory committee identify the program objectives that will receive primary attention during a specified length of time and then develop a plan for implementation. The strategies or methods are the means of achieving the program objectives and vary based on the ability and/or grade level of the user and the classroom curriculum. Let us assume that a priority is to provide daily opportunities for students to browse, explore, and use all the resources of the library media center. Several strategies for achieving this objective might be set in motion:

1. Every teacher will have a method in place that will give individual students access to the library media center at many times during the school day.

2. The library media center will have activities available for individual students at all times, such as individual learning centers, pillows for relaxed reading, an area for quiet study or research, audiovisual production centers, and free-choice use of books and audiovisual and computer media.

3. The library media center facilities will be arranged so that individuals going in and out of the library media center will not disturb small and large groups working in the center.

4. Students will be taught the variety of options they have when they come to the library media center as well as how to pursue their needs and interests independently of the library media center staff.

Policies and Procedures

Strategies that are envisioned will need to be framed as policies and procedures to be applied to all faculty and students. While the library media specialist may have all these procedures in mind, it is best to have them written down so that everyone understands how the library media center operates. The move from a limited access program to a flexible access program requires that all policies and procedures be reviewed. Policies that were adequate for a traditional program may indeed inhibit access and should be discarded. Policies and procedures should emphasize the ownership of the library media program by staff, students, and parents. To encourage access to resources and facilities, library media center rules and regulations should be few and flexible, simple and self-explanatory. For example, a simple pass system might allow classroom teachers the flexibility to send students, either in small groups or individually, for practical application of skills through browsing, circulation, listening and viewing, research, and centers.

The policies and procedures of the library media center might be divided into four categories: (1) access to facilities; (2) access to resources; (3) access to personnel; and (4) access to instruction. Possible policy statements and the reasoning behind them should be carefully considered before the actual statements are written and adopted. Following are some sample policy statements in these four areas and some of the reasons behind them:

Access to Facilities
Students and staff have access to the library media center any day, every day and anytime throughout the day. The library media center is open before school, after school, and continuously throughout the day.

The arrangement of the library media center should allow simultaneous use by all grade levels. Allow small groups and individuals to enter the library media center at any time. The use of a library media pass allows the teacher to specify the length of time and indicate the independent task (see figure 3.3). It is not unusual for several fifth-grade students to be working on a reference assignment, a small group of first graders to be compiling a picture dictionary, and the library media specialist to be instructing a fourth-grade class on using a microcomputer database, while a kindergarten class checks out books.

Listening, viewing, large-group instruction, small-group activities, computer use, and circulation may all occur at the same time and therefore need designated areas.

The traffic pattern should allow children freedom of movement to all areas of the media center without disrupting other activities.

Several years ago, as we surveyed our recently rearranged media center, a colleague of mine remarked: "You're the only person I know who has a reason for having each piece of furniture in a particular spot." I laughed and then began to enumerate the reasons for placing some of the items in their current positions. I learned long ago that the arrangement of the library media center can either encourage or impede flexible access.

Explore various arrangements for simultaneous activity so that in scheduling you are aware of what activities can occur at the same time. One of the facilities for our flexible access program also served as the school auditorium. Each time there was a program the custodian would dutifully move all the furniture to allow seating of half the student body. At the conclusion of the program, as he prepared to return the furniture, he would invariably ask: "Where do you want me to put these tables?" I consistently responded that it didn't matter, knowing that the first time I had an activity scheduled the furniture would be rearranged.

Finally, realizing the custodian's frustration because the principal had directed him to "put the media center back like it was," I made a map for him to use to put us back in order. Within minutes, as I prepared for a scheduled activity, I had us "out of order."

Access to Resources
Materials are classified, cataloged, housed, and circulated for easy retrieval.

An accurate, efficient procedure for signing items in and out of the library media center enhances the flexible access library media program. An automated circulation system is valuable, but if that is not possible, a simple manual circulation system run principally by students might be of value. A description of one manual system is given in appendix G.

The procedure in some flexible access library media programs is for circulation to be unscheduled. Students are sent to the library media center to browse when their work is completed or when they have finished a book and have it in hand to be returned. With this approach it is easy for the less diligent and responsible students to miss library media experiences. Teachers who have little time for instruction with their entire class because of the number of students participating in various special programs are often reluctant to provide another activity that takes children away from the classroom. They find that when extra time is needed it is convenient to postpone individual checkout. It is important that the library media program procedures ensure students time to circulate materials a minimum of once per week and that students and staff have opportunities to check out materials every day, as often as they wish.

Fig. 3.3. Media Pass.

Some flexible access library media programs have found that teacher-generated circulation schedules are very successful. Such schedules tend to lessen teacher anxiety by establishing a book checkout and return routine. Parents are less apprehensive about the flexible access program when the classroom teacher establishes a specific book return day or book return routine. Developing such a schedule does not negate spontaneous use of the library media center. Students are encouraged to use the library media center before and after school and anytime during the day; teachers are encouraged to schedule a time so that the students have continual access. Teacher-developed circulation schedules may provide various options, with varying responsibilities for each option. Attach an explanation of the options to the schedule for reference when scheduling (see figure 3.4). The times available for checkout are determined by the library media specialist, the time for each class is determined by the teacher. The library media specialist provides a blank schedule and teachers schedule as appropriate for their classes.

Since this policy does not affect the library media specialist's time, the teacher is responsible for the noise level, straightening of the library media center, and assisting in student book selection. Should a scheduling conflict arise, it is the teacher's responsibility to reschedule the class. Small groups may be sent to the library media center for checkout on successive days or for successive times. For example, students from Mrs. Smith's class may come to the library media center in small groups Mondays through Fridays at 11:00 or small groups may rotate through on Wednesdays from 9:30 to 11:00.

Teachers who use learning centers in the classroom often have as the "fifth" center for the week small group checkout or have a reading group checkout while one reading group does seat work and the other group works with the teacher. Circulation individually or by pairs functions the same way. The teacher indicates on the schedule either that students will be checking out at various times throughout the week or the times students will be coming individually or in pairs. Small-group and individual circulation is supervised by the library media aide. If there is no assistant, the schedule framework would then reflect those times when the library media specialist is available to supervise circulation. Other activities would be scheduled accordingly. Figure 3.5 provides a sample of a student checkout schedule which has been filled in by teachers.

Access to Personnel
The work schedule for the library media staff ensures access to personnel during all hours of operation.

Duty for media personnel should be full-time in the media center and not elsewhere in the school. The job descriptions, duties, and responsibilities for the library media staff should reflect the flexible access philosophy. For example, our goal of developing independent library media users influenced the decision that no staff member or volunteer would be assigned to the circulation desk. All students circulate their own materials, whether manually or by computer. Encouraging independence in the library media center allows the library media specialist time to help teachers teach and students learn.

Fig. 3.4. Sample Memo to Teachers from Library Media Specialist.

TO: ALL CLASSROOM TEACHERS

FROM: YOUR LIBRARY MEDIA SPECIALIST

RE: SCHEDULING STUDENT CHECKOUT

Please sign up for a checkout time for your students. You currently have three options available. You may:

1.   Send students individually throughout a day or the week.

2.   Send small groups throughout a day or the week.

3.   Accompany your entire class once a week.

For small group or class checkout, fill in your name in each day(s) desired time and indicate the group size (S = small group or C = class) on the attached schedule. We can accommodate three small groups during each time slot or one large group.

If you will be sending students individually throughout a particular day, indicate the beginning time on that day with your name and an "I" for individual. Should you elect to send students individually throughout the *week* please indicate by placing your name at the bottom of the sheet.

Please let me know if you have any questions regarding the scheduling or if you have an additional option to suggest. I am enclosing a media pass form for your use.

Fig. 3.5. Student Checkout Schedule.

	MONDAY	TUESDAY	WEDNESDAY	THURSDAY	FRIDAY
9:30		Cobb 2nd S	Beckner 2nd S	Stewart 2nd S	
10:00	Swenson 2nd S	Cobb 2nd S / Roof 2nd S	Beckner 2nd S / Burns 2nd S / McGhee 2nd S	Stewart 2nd S / Boothe 2nd S	VanDyne Kdg. C
10:30	Swenson 2nd S	Cobb 2nd S / Roof 2nd S	Beckner 2nd S / Burns 2nd S / McGhee 1st S	Stewart 2nd S / Boothe 2nd S	
11:00	Swenson 2nd S / Thomas 5th S	Roof 2nd S / Thomas 5th S	Burns 2nd S / McGhee 1st S / Thomas 5th S	Boothe 2nd S	
11:30		Charlton Kdg. C	Campbell 1st C		Gourden 3rd C
12:00	Barnes 1st C	Hine 1st C			
12:30	Kemp 4th S	Hanberry 4th S		C.homtas 1st C	
1:00	Kemp 4th S	Hanberry 4th S	Guppy 4th C	McGaughey 4th C	Foster Kdg. C
1:30	Albury Kdg. C	Koepke Kdg. C	Stewart Kdg. C	Paul Kdg. C	Rusho 1st C
2:00	Baker Kdg. S / Wright 4th S	Baker Kdg. S / Wright 4th	Baker Kdg. S / Wright 4th S	Baker Kdg. S / Wright 4th S	Baker Kdg. S / Wright 4th S

Individual Monday through Friday: Whitney 3rd, Blomeley 3rd, Bowdoin 3rd, High 3rd, Durak 5th, Thomas 5th.

Key: S = Small group visits   C = Class group visits   I = Individual visits

Access to Instruction
Teachers and library media specialists plan instruction both in content areas and in library/information skills as required by the classroom curriculum and at times when learning is likely to be enhanced.

The portion of the library media policy addressing instruction needs to encompass who will be providing instruction, what instruction will be provided, and why. The procedures explain how instruction is scheduled. Instruction delivered by the library media specialist follows a predetermined scope and sequence for information skills. Instruction is scheduled by the library media specialist and the teacher after cooperative planning and takes precedence over other requests. Classes are not scheduled on a regular basis but as needed. A teacher does not routinely have instruction on a particular day at a particular time (e.g., Monday at 9:00) but may choose to schedule a unit of instruction that covers several weeks for successive Mondays at 9:00 if that slot is not already scheduled by another teacher. Or the teacher, after planning with the library media specialist, may schedule instruction in the library media center each day at 9:00 for a week or more. The frequency of instruction is flexible and so is the length of each instructional period. The library media specialist and teacher determine the length of time for each lesson.

Students may be scheduled for unit activities in large groups, small groups, or individually. Address the procedure for scheduling each group in the procedures manual. Generally only one group is scheduled for unit work with the library media specialist at a time, but other groups and individuals will be using the library media center simultaneously. Individual students needing assistance with a particular project or activity should be scheduled. For large groups or whole class activities, the teacher remains with the class to share the teaching and supervision of the class. The teacher's presence and participation in library media activities makes it possible for two adults to work together to ensure that the activity is successful. The means for tracking activities also needs to be determined. The library media specialist may use a lesson plan book or calendar to record individual, small-group and large-group activities.

EIGHT MAJOR SUGGESTIONS

During the design phase for flexible access programs each library media program's goals, objectives, policies, and procedures must fit the overall pattern and philosophy of the school. Development of these categories with a faculty will create a situation of ownership and pride of program. Since designing a unique flexible access program for each school is a challenge, following are eight major suggestions for the library media specialist to consider as the design is planned, proposed, and executed.

Know Your Information Skills Curriculum

A thorough knowledge of the information skills curriculum is necessary to maintain the focus not only for skills instruction but also for all other library media experiences. The library media specialist and the teacher divide the responsibility for teaching the content of the unit and including appropriate information skills required by that content. For example, to teach a third-grade unit on the solar system, the library media specialist might teach accessing information using the table of contents and indexes of books on the planets (information skills) while the teacher covers the order of the planets (content skill). The roles might be reversed, or both aspects taught jointly.

Relevant skills instruction is provided by following a scope and sequence of media or information skills that has been developed for the individual school. A number of printed scope and sequence charts are available from school districts, state departments of education, and from articles in the literature. If a scope and sequence document is to be created, readers might consult Mancall, Aaron, and Walker's six-step curriculum revision process, which examines the existing information skills program in relation to critical thinking skills.

The following four-step process is a simple method of scope and sequence construction:

1. Provide a list of skills, by grade, to the appropriate teachers and ask them to react to them. This initial list should be based on the county or district curriculum and/or the state scope and sequence, if available. Information skills are not only locational skills but also literature appreciation skills. Major skill areas generally addressed in an information skills scope and sequence are (a) literary, (b) media production, (c) listening and viewing, (d) information analysis, (e) critical thinking, and (f) communication of information.

2. Have the teachers in the grade level either above or below each grade provide feedback on the lists submitted.

3. Submit a rough draft of the skills continuum to all teachers. Ask them to respond to the draft.

4. Submit the final draft of the information skills scope and sequence to the staff for endorsement.

Involving teachers in this process will make them more eager participants in cooperative planning and integration of these skills into unit content. Teachers will be aware of the information skills for their particular grade level and will have already begun to assume ownership of the flexible access library media program.

Know Your School Curriculum

Since the need for information skills arises only as children are studying curricular subjects, it is imperative that the library media specialist become an active participant in the school's curriculum prior to implementation of a flexible access program. Curricular awareness is developed in a variety of ways:

1. *Attending curriculum committee meetings.* As specific strategies for teaching curriculum are discussed, the library media specialist is able to identify ways to assist. For example, as the language arts committee discusses student publishing guidelines, the library media specialist may suggest that lessons be developed to introduce publication terminology to the various grade levels.

2. *Studying curriculum guides and textbooks.* Maintain a complete set of teacher's editions and curriculum guides in the library media center's professional collection. First examine the overview in the various textbooks or guides used in all grade levels. The library media specialist whose school uses the reading textbook series that has stated its major goal as "to develop independent readers who will use reading in a lifetime pursuit of learning and enjoyment" has good evidence for the need for flexible access. All one needs to do is substitute the term *library media users* for *readers*.

   Preview the textbooks or curriculum guides in light of the curriculum content, the information skills included in the text, and ideas for resource-based teaching. Review the table of contents, acknowledgments, and illustrations to prepare a list for each grade level of subject areas that lend themselves to resource-based teaching and in which information skills might be particularly relevant. Such a list might include: (a) existing units from previous years that can be adapted to the new approach, (b) authors/illustrators whose works you know and enjoy that are featured in the text, (c) literary genres recommended in the text, and (d) themes that are "naturals" for integration with the curriculum. This list then forms the basis for an initial cooperative planning session with a single teacher or for a single grade level.

   For each resource-based topical study, create a bibliography of library media center materials. An electronic catalog makes this an easy task. Items related to specific units can be coded in a computer field by text and grade level for instant retrieval.

3. *Visiting the classrooms.* Bulletin boards suggest a teacher's individual curriculum and priorities. A teacher who is highlighting an author or a particular subject in a display is the perfect candidate for suggesting related media experiences. Teachers who use supplementary classroom paperback sets in teaching reading will most likely be receptive to cooperatively planned literature and whole language activities.

4. *Reviewing purchase requests.* Useful information can be gleaned from reviewing teacher requests for purchase of materials. These requests often indicate the "hidden" curriculum: those activities teachers *choose* to do rather than *have* to do.

5. *Designing and distributing yearly and grading period planning sheets* (see figure 4.3 on page 62).

Know Your Teachers

Seek those teachers who have shown support of the library media program and begin to plan with them. This might be an entire grade level with whom you have established a special rapport, a department, or individual teachers. It is wise to ally yourself with teachers who have initiated ideas for cooperative activities within the fixed library media schedule or with those who have shown an openness to new ideas. A note of caution though: support of the library media specialist as an individual does not ensure support of the role of the library media specialist in a flexible access library media program. One of my dearest colleagues commented on an evaluation prior to implementation of our flexible access program that she and her teammates wanted "a full year course of study of library skills with book checkout at the end of each lesson." This was not the teacher nor the grade on which I concentrated my efforts during the initial implementation of the program! Initially the lessons planned with the supportive teachers were taught within the fixed schedule. The following year, with a nucleus of accepting and supporting teachers, I was able to focus my energies on the more reluctant members of the staff.

Take opportunities to observe in the classrooms. What teaching strategies do the teachers use? If manipulatives are used in a classroom, that teacher will probably respond to student activity centers in the media center. The teacher with a textbook-dominated curriculum will probably accept the idea of activities that reinforce the text. How are the students grouped? If the teacher provides the majority of instruction in large groups, then the library media specialist will initially want to suggest large-group activities. The teacher who has established a routine of small-group instruction and experiences will be more likely to pursue activities in the library media center.

Informal conversations with teachers can provide useful insight. Talk in the teacher's lounge often centers on special activities or problems in the classroom. The observant library media specialist can follow up on these with suggestions for library media program correlations or file the idea for future use with a particular teacher.

Noticing what materials, equipment, and services the teachers request and what the teachers and their students borrow can provide an indication of approaches that will be effective with a particular teacher. A teacher who frequently uses videotapes for science instruction can easily be encouraged to plan activities with the library media specialist to use Reading Rainbow videotapes correlated with the science program. Does the demand for holiday materials exceed the supply each season? Plan appropriate primary and intermediate centers or activities in the library media center and make them available to all students and teachers.

Notice the students who use the library media center. What kind of assignments do they do in the media center? Are there prerequisite skills you could offer to introduce to the class before they begin working on the teacher's yearly encyclopedia worksheet? Are students asked to locate books for genre book reports? Suggest that the introduction to the characteristics of a particular genre occur in the library media center. Which teachers send students to the library media center for "free" time? These teachers might welcome cooperatively planned recreational reading activities in the library media center.

Know Your Students

The library media specialist not only needs superior knowledge of library and information science but also knowledge of the way children learn. A rigid schedule often necessitates class visits where students are taught as a whole. Flexible access allows teaching to be student-centered and to occur through various instructional modes: large-group, small-group, and individual. The varying ability levels, personalities, and interests of students are considered and activities are provided that incorporate all learning modalities. Active participation in learning is encouraged. Students are given the opportunity to practice information and production skills and assume responsibility for learning through self-directed and self-paced activities.

Professional reading and observation in the classroom reveal that successful teaching methods used in primary grades incorporate hands-on learning, physical activity, language development, and socialization. Experience will confirm that the same methods are effective with all elementary students. Brainstorm with students about memorable learning experiences and good teachers. Why were they memorable? What are the common denominators? These will probably include doing, not sitting; choice of activity; a tangible end product; having every student involved; and teamwork activity.

Once you know what makes learning exciting and relevant for your students, plan lessons and experiences accordingly. In my own library media center, a media scavenger hunt used for fourth- and fifth-grade student orientation always has the children clamoring to do it again. This activity involves every student in locating and manipulating materials in all areas of the library media center and sharing the excitement and the task with a partner.

Know Your Collection

Familiarize yourself with your library media collection in relation to curricular objectives, the goals established for the library media program, and the teaching strategies employed in your school. Order materials and equipment based on the strengths and weaknesses you observe. Solicite staff input for selection, preview, and weeding of materials. One of the first activities in which the staff of my school was involved (after moving to my "new" school built in 1928 and finding a collection dating to that time) was an all-day "garden party." Guidelines for weeding were reviewed and each teacher assumed responsibility for removing from a particular section those items that met the established criteria. They were instructed to indicate titles that they wished replaced and to offer suggestions for expanding that portion of the collection. I was delighted when the physical education teacher spent his entire planning period offering suggestions for the 700s and biographies. He may have been enticed to the library media center for the refreshments, but after tasting the array of fruits and vegetables, he easily accomplished what would have taken me much time and deliberation to do. It was then a simple task to review those items the teachers had selected for discard, make the final decisions, and begin an order for new materials. That one activity not only assisted in updating the collection but also assured that the staff acquire an investment in the library media program.

Organize Your Materials into Curriculum Areas

Flexible access library media programs require both creativity and organizational skills. First focus on organization, later on creativity. (Refer to appendix E for a list of publishers of ideas for units.) Do not throw away the instructional materials you used in a fixed schedule or rush to create new materials. Instead, revamp or reorganize the materials you presently use so that they can be inserted into existing areas of the curriculum. A fellow library media specialist commented to me that she was almost ready to begin flexible access but that she had to make centers first. I realized then that she thought a flexible access library media program required making centers. Centers have proven to be an integral component of my program because I am comfortable teaching with and providing reinforcement through centers, but other library media specialists must use those strategies with which they are most comfortable. It is possible to have a successful flexible access library media center program that does not incorporate library media specialist-produced centers.

Organize your files to correlate with the curriculum so that (1) materials can be pulled at a moment's notice, (2) materials or units may be used to show other teachers, and (3) materials can be used in subsequent years. I have found it useful to organize materials by subject in what I call *box units*. These topical treasure boxes (both large and small) are homemade kits with all kinds of goodies likely to be used in a unit of instruction.

Although a new basal reading series is adopted in our district every five years and new curricula emerge, I am confident that at some point in the primary curriculum the same subjects I am currently teaching will be included. These topics are the basis for my primary box units. Any suggestions for activities or materials related to one of the units that crosses my desk goes in the appropriate box. During cooperative planning sessions the teachers enjoy as much as I do searching the contents of a related box to locate lesson ideas for a specific topic. Relevant activities are selected from the box for each occasion. One year kindergarten children may use farm animal stencils to make an ABC book to reinforce alphabetical order skills, while the following year the same stencils may be used during the farm unit to reinforce sequencing.

The box units for intermediate grades focus on literary genre. I am certain that the intermediate curriculum at some point also includes historical fiction, folktales, science fiction, and so forth. These boxes are pulled when appropriate to integrate skills in social studies, science, or any area of the curriculum.

I also organize materials in planning notebooks. These notebooks contain excerpts from text overviews relating to information skills, bibliographies from the text checked against the collection, subject lists, planning sheets, previous cooperatively planned lessons, and display sketches (refer to chapter 4).

Educate Your Teachers

Once the library media specialist is prepared, the education of teachers can begin. The approaches to use in educating teachers in the flexible access library media program concept should be determined by the principal and library media specialist. The commitment of the principal and library media specialist are crucial to the initial implementation of the program. The commitment of the teachers is crucial to the survival and success of the program. In educating teachers, it is necessary to remember that they will not be eager to pledge support to a program they do not understand and have not seen. The first focus should be on changing teacher attitudes, followed by a change in practices. Teachers used to a rigid access program have been conditioned to believe that library media lessons should be taught once a week; in thirty- to forty-five-minute sessions; by the library media specialist with no involvement in planning, prelearning, or follow-up activities by the classroom teacher; or using the one lesson, one skill approach.

One method of changing staff perceptions is to engage in a program of staff development. However, the mere mention of another staff meeting or staff training session may create a great deal of resentment. Staff development research conducted by Fullan identified several reasons for the failure of traditional staff development methods:

1. Preponderance of one-shot workshops.

2. Failure to provide follow-up for individual teachers.

3. Failure to address individual needs and concerns.

4. Failure to provide building level support for the new skills.[7]

Therefore, an effective flexible access teacher education plan should follow these guidelines:

1. Each training session or in-service needs to be short and to the point. The attention span of teachers at the end of the day is limited.

2. Training should be continual, not confined to one session or one day. A series of sessions during which teachers have an opportunity to try and to discuss techniques is crucial. Several media blitzes scheduled during the year can also be quite effective. Children's Book Week and National Library Week offer occasions to bring forward the flexible access library media program. Participation can be encouraged in "free" storytimes for each of the grade levels. A short article in the faculty newsletter or library media memo can expound upon this service and how teachers can obtain it.

3. A combination of approaches, mediums, and methods (training sessions, sharing sessions, one-to-one assistance, and meetings) should be used. Joyce and Showers found that to effect a change in practice, professional development should include theory, demonstration, practice with feedback, and application with coaching.[8]

4. The benefits of participating in the training should be obvious to the teacher. The in-service should focus on specific job-related tasks unique to the school.

5. New teacher and student orientation is provided as necessary to allow for participants at different cognition and experience levels.

6. The in-service is flexible to change and grow with the program.

Probably the most efficient and effective means of introducing the concept of flexible access is the general faculty meeting. The library media specialist has a captive audience, the teachers generally appear receptive because the principal is present, and all teachers are receiving the same information at the same time rather than having it skewed by being disseminated through other staff members. A usually crowded agenda and insufficient time for adequate presentations limit the use of this approach for subsequent sessions.

In my case, with only a few days of school remaining, the principal informed me that I was to explain flexible scheduling to the teachers on one of the last days of post-school planning. The teachers would be voting afterward and would be encouraged to include comments on their ballots. I was horrified. I was not a salesperson; couldn't the principal just tell them we would be trying the approach next fall? He was aware then of what I am certain of now, that in order for us to effect change, the teachers had to be a part of the decision-making process.

At that time many of our teachers were enrolled in graduate programs and had confided to me the difficulty they were having with locating resources and in using the university library. Many of them were currently students and could therefore readily identify with the frustrations of our students. This proved to be an excellent introduction for the services that would emanate from curriculum-integrated media skills instruction in our school. I followed with specific examples of how recent activities generated in the classroom could be taught effectively using multiple resources and could also be naturals for integrated information skills instruction. I had developed laryngitis over the weekend and when I finally whispered my last words the time of reckoning had arrived. The emphasis was on what students and teachers would be receiving through the program rather than on what the teachers were losing. Many of the teachers expressed dislike of losing the break time afforded by the library media specialist, but the teachers unanimously agreed that our primary concern should be the benefits to students. The integration of skills through a more flexible schedule was what was needed to prepare our students to be independent media users. I like to think that my arguments were so convincing that there was no choice in how the teachers would vote, but from their expressions I think some were sympathy votes from my presenting in a whisper. I'll never know what swayed them, so just to be safe you might want to contract laryngitis before a presentation to an unreceptive faculty!

It is more difficult to present the flexible access concept to your own faculty than to other people. Leeds has listed three fears that all speakers share: fear of performing poorly, fear of the audience, or fear that their material is not good enough.[9] She offers suggestions for combating those fears, which can be applied to a faculty presentation on flexible access library media programs. You will have every reason to be confident if you remember:

1. *To carefully prepare your presentation.* Keep in mind the purpose of your presentation. What do you want the teachers to do, know, or feel at the conclusion of your presentation? Use point-example-point to describe what, when, where, how much, how often, and why.

2. *Who your audience is and what their interest in the topic is.* You are able to tell your listeners something that is really worth your time and theirs. Use persuasive words such as *discover, easy, proven*, and *results*.

   A. *Discover*—Telling teachers that you want to share a discovery with them makes your enthusiasm contagious.

   B. *Easy*—With so many demands on teacher's time, the mention of something quick and uncomplicated will be welcome.

   C. *Proven*—Teachers feel more confident when told that the program has been tested and given approval by others.

   D. *Results*—Let them know what they will get and what will happen.

3. Use the word *you*—*your* session and *your* class rather than *today's* session or *I*.[10]

Personalize or custom design the flexible access introductory presentation for each particular staff. Use the information you have gleaned about teachers' interests (both personal and professional) and their teaching styles to design the presentation. In my case, conversations with staff members had made me aware of teacher involvement in continuing education. When designing an in-service for the staff in the school in which she taught, Terry Campanella capitalized on having been one of them and focused on the benefits of a flexible access program for those particular teachers. She assessed the current status of the media program and emphasized positive actions for those areas that she considered as potential problems. A clever read-aloud script and simple graphics created by Terry is provided in appendix C.

All outlines for flexible access staff presentations should:

1. State the goal of your program and ask for support.

2. Give a specific objective.

3. Conclude by enumerating ways the teachers can assist in achieving the objective. Explain what they are expected to do with the information. Ask them to either act on your ideas by doing something specific or think about your ideas.

Cooperative planning is often a mystery, especially in schools where each classroom is a separate entity and planning is done individually rather than as a team. To relieve the anxiety that teachers feel about the initial planning session, plan a short in-service. In such an instance the outline for the faculty presentation might be as follows:

1. Explain why cooperative planning should occur in your school. Mention student benefits, but concentrate on teacher benefits. Emphasize that by pooling your efforts through cooperative planning the curriculum will become more manageable. Cooperative planning is *not* an additional burden for teachers to assume, but rather an opportunity to have assistance in teaching their curriculum.

2. State your goal: Each class will have one cooperatively planned media experience within the next two months.

3. Ask that the teachers schedule a convenient time within the next two weeks for a cooperative planning session.

4. Request that the planning sheet be completed prior to the scheduled planning session.

5. Role play a planning session. (Choose a supportive teacher to assist you in the preparation of this portion of the in-service. Rehearse the behaviors you wish to be illustrated in your role playing and provide each teacher with a copy of the completed planning sheet that you are using during the mock planning session.)

Videotape faculty presentations; they can be used for new teacher orientation.

After the initial introduction of the program to all teachers, presentations to curriculum committees or grade levels are effective. Use other means of communicating in conjunction with the large-group and small-group presentations. The methods of communicating with teachers and administrators should be simple in order to ensure continued and continual use:

1. *Newsletters*. Newsletters, generated either by the media center or the administrative office, are a perfect means of educating staff on a regular basis. Successful flexible access experiences initiated by the teachers could be highlighted in a "recognition" column in the staff newsletter. Not only is this good for public relations, but it is often the stimulus for other teachers to relate their unique experiences. A newsletter published by the media staff might regularly include suggested seasonal and school-wide activities and an annotated list of new and seasonal materials. Each issue might focus on a different area of the curriculum and provide ideas for integrating information skills into that particular subject.

2. *Reprints*. Several schools have reprinted an article by Carolyn Durak (appendix D), which chronicles the emotions of a classroom teacher during the implementation of a flexible access library media program in her school. Others have shared the article with teachers during faculty meetings.

3. *Displays*. Subliminal education occurs through displays and bulletin boards. When designing our new media center, I purposely located the professional library and conference room, where cooperative planning sessions occur, so that teachers must walk through the media center past bulletin boards and display areas.

4. *Conversation.* The most frequent form of education is the informal conversation between library media specialist and teacher or between teacher and teacher. The education of some of my most reluctant teachers has been brought about by another teacher of a different grade level in the staff dining room. Advocates of flexible access library media programs become experts at interjecting the concept of the program into any conversation.

5. *Personalized services.* Individualized bibliographies for teachers are a simple but effective means for educating teachers and garnering support for your flexible access program. Physical education teachers are most receptive to bibliographies of titles that encourage movement. Provide suggestions to teachers showing how books can be used to simplify the writing of inclement weather plans. Personalizing the media program for each teacher provides a powerful illustration of the benefits of a flexible access library media program.

6. *Observation.* Invite teachers to observe classes in the media center. By observing different grades or other classes in their grade the teachers are able to see the program in action.

7. *Public address announcements and school news broadcasts.* Show clips of various media activities at each grade level.

8. *Advertisements.* Announce a new product or service. Place a book cart with seasonal titles for checkout in the teachers' lounge. Attach a sign: "Check with the library media specialist for additional titles and to plan related activities."

9. *Planning sessions.* Each scheduled planning session with teachers provides an opportunity to further educate. The cooperative planning time scheduled with all teachers meets the requirements for effective training. The sessions are short and to the point, continuous, and demonstrate benefits obvious to the teacher.

The key to a successful teacher education program is to use every opportunity and every conceivable strategy to maintain constant visibility of the program.

It is important that teachers experience ownership and feel a part of the decision-making process, but do not actually seek their permission. The better approach is to ask for teachers' support for a trial period. Begin the trial period at the start of the school year rather than later when classroom schedules and routines would be disrupted. The trial should last long enough for the library media specialist to adequately educate the staff, for teachers to participate in several cooperative planning sessions, and for both parties to observe the results of their efforts.

Conduct a Status Evaluation

The process of evaluating the program components should occur in the design phase as well as during the actual implementation. Review each segment of this chapter to see if your flexible access program includes those facets that will contribute to a successful program. After the program has begun, check up often. Are policies and procedures working? Are objectives being met? For example, when evaluating the objective "Provide daily opportunities for students to browse, explore, and use all resources of the media center," the evaluation objectives and indicators would be as follows:

Objective	Indicator
Full access	Hours of operation
	Evidence that students have maximum access to all media
	Circulation rules encourage, not discourage use
Full attendance	Numbers of students in attendance
	All grade levels represented
	Types of groups coming to the center
	Simultaneous activities scheduled

Note those items that need improvement. To determine priorities, consider how essential an item is to the success of your particular flexible access library media program. This same evaluation may be used at specific intervals for total program evaluation.

Consider internal and external factors that may keep the library media program goals from being attained. Assess the strong points and positive attributes of the current program.

Perhaps a checklist can help, noting items that are just beginning, those in operation, and those that still need attention. Figure 3.6 provides such a checklist which can be adapted to local use.

Fig. 3.6. Flexible Access Design Checklist.

Date _____

Indicate for each of the items below the response that most accurately reflects the current status of your library media program design.

	In Place and Working	Beginning to Work	Needs Help
1. Goals and objectives			
2. Policies and procedures reflect flexible access philosophy			
3. Facilities arranged for flexible access			
4. Circulation system			
5. Knowledge of school's curriculum			
6. Familiarity with textbooks			
7. Familiarity with teaching styles of your teachers			
8. Written list of services			
9. Teacher/library media specialist planning schedule			
10. Use of cooperative planning sheet			
11. Cooperative planning sessions			
12. Use of scope and sequence of information skills			

13. Tracking system for what skills are taught, to whom, and when

14. Information skills instruction related to classroom activities

15. Simultaneous use of the media center for a variety of activities and by different age levels

16. Individual use of the media center

17. Small-group use of the media center

18. Large-group/class use of the media center

19. Print and nonprint collection for resource based units

20. Organization of teaching materials for easy access and curriculum integration

21. Teacher preparation/introduction to the flexible access library media program

22. Teacher/student handbooks

23. Communication with administrators

24. Methods of program evaluation

COMMENTS AND SUGGESTIONS:

PROFESSIONAL ACTIVITIES

1. Complete the "So You Want to Be Flexible" test (appendix B).

2. Determine goals and objectives for your flexible access library media program.

3. Prepare a list of services for teachers and for students.

4. Write or rewrite policies and procedures to reflect the goals and objectives of your flexible access program.

5. Determine a curriculum entry point for each grade.

6. Outline a plan for designing your flexible access library media program.

7. Develop an action plan for designing your flexible access library media program.

8. Evaluate the current status of your program using the Flexible Access Design Checklist (figure 3.6). Prioritize those areas you have indicated need improvement, then develop a plan for improving the high priority areas.

NOTES

[1]Kathy Kren (library media specialist, Bennett Park Montessori Center, Buffalo, New York), response to questionnaire from author, 1990.

[2]Ibid.

[3]Marlene Lazzara (library media specialist, Henking Elementary School, Glenview, Illinois), response to questionnaire from author, 1990.

[4]Nell Brown (library media specialist, Wadsworth Elementary School, Palm Coast, Florida), response to questionnaire from author, 1990.

[5]Jo Ann Gadicke (library media specialist, Cheboygan, Wisconsin), response to questionnaire from author, 1990.

[6]Jacqueline C. Mancall, Shirley L. Aaron, and Sue A. Walker, "Educating Students to Think: The Role of the Library Media Program: A Concept Paper Written for the National Commission on Libraries and Information Science," *School Library Media Quarterly* 15 (Fall 1986): 18-27.

[7]M. Fullan, *The Meaning of Educational Change* (New York: Teachers College Press, 1982).

[8]B. R. Joyce and B. Showers, "The Coaching of Teaching," *Educational Leadership* 40, no. 2: 4-10.

[9]Dorothy Leeds, *Powerspeak: The Complete Guide to Persuasive Public Speaking and Presenting* (New York: Prentice Hall, 1988).

[10]Ibid.

ADDITIONAL READINGS

Barth, Roland S. "Principals, Teachers, and School Leadership." *Phi Delta Kappan* (May 1988): 639-42.

Duff, Ann. "Who Cares If There's an Open Schedule?" *Florida Media Quarterly* 14 (Fall 1988): 7.
    A district media supervisor writes an open letter to a principal who wants to improve his library media program.

Haycock, Carol-Ann. "Developing the School Resource Centre Program: A Systematic Approach." *Emergency Librarian* (September/October 1984): 9-16.
    A valuable contribution to flexible access literature, this article outlines and gives specific ideas for developing a library media program with cooperative planning as the core.

Hodges, Gerald G. "Educating School Media Professionals to Perform Their Instructional Role." In *School Library Media Annual* edited by Elwood E. Miller, 3: 165-76. Littleton, Colo.: Libraries Unlimited, 1985.

Kulleseid, Eleanor R. "The Leadership Role of the Library Media Specialist: Some Humanistic Models of Cooperation." In *School Library Media Annual*, edited by Shirley L. Aaron and Pat Scales, 5: 155-66, Littleton, Colo.: Libraries Unlimited, 1987.

Leggett, Diana, and Sharon Hoyle. "Peer Coaching: One District's Experience in Using Teachers as Staff Developers." *Journal of Staff Development* 8 (Spring 1987): 37-41.

Liesener, James A. *A Systematic Process for Planning Media Programs.* Chicago: American Library Association, 1976.

Loertscher, David V. "Information Skills for Children and Young Adults: START NOW!" *School Library Media Activities Monthly* 1 (December 1984): 30-34.

Markuson, Carolyn. "Making It Happen: Taking Charge of the Information Curriculum." *School Library Media Quarterly* 14 (Fall 1986): 37-47.

Shaw, Mabel W. "Planning Effective Library Media Programs: Liesener Revisited." In *School Library Media Annual*, edited by Elwood E. Miller, 4: 208-18, Littleton, Colo.: Libraries Unlimited, 1986.

Turner, Philip M. "In-service and the School Library Media Specialist: What Works and What Doesn't." *School Library Media Quarterly* 16 (Winter 1988): 106-9.

Chapter 4

Cooperative Planning
The Essential Element in Your Flexible Access Library Media Program

This chapter provides information to assist the library media specialist in:

1. identifying the composition of cooperative planning teams,

2. designing cooperative planning tools, and

3. creating cooperatively planned lessons or units.

Once the library media specialist is prepared and organized for flexible access and has introduced the staff to the philosophy, work as a team can begin. Cooperative planning builds on the strengths of each member of the educational team. Figure 4.1 illustrates what will happen in cooperative planning sessions as the teacher and the library media specialist sit down to prepare a resource-based teaching unit.

Cooperative planning often occurs in the staff lounge or when staff members pass each other in the hallway; they are planning opportunities that should not be overlooked. However, the success of the program relies on formal, scheduled planning time with teachers. The most frequent complaint of educators is that there is neither enough time nor enough help to accomplish their myriad of tasks. Time is valuable for the classroom teacher and for the library media specialist, and if left to chance, cooperative planning is often last on the list of priorities. It is essential to the success of a flexible access library media program that planning occur on a regular basis during formally scheduled planning times.

Fig. 4.1. Cooperative Planning Session Model.

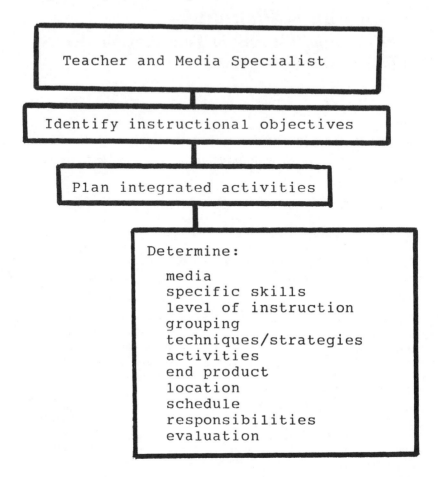

PLANNING SCHEDULE WITH TEACHERS

Time for planning will be scheduled if it is a high priority with the library media specialist and if teachers have input in developing the schedule. The library media specialist prepares the framework for the schedule and the teachers determine (1) the time for cooperative planning, (2) who will participate, (3) the frequency of meetings, and (4) their duration. An ordinary monthly calendar can be used to schedule meetings (see figure 4.2). The library media specialist needs uninterrupted time with the teachers, time that does not interfere with the library media center routine. Teachers may choose before and after student school hours, contractual planning time, or workdays. Scheduling sessions before school ensures that the actual planning does not extend beyond the time allotted, but it often results in teachers having to return during their class planning time to complete the session. After-school meetings sometimes start slowly and then turn into marathon sessions.

Fig. 4.2. Cooperative Planning Schedule.

MONDAY	TUESDAY	WEDNESDAY	THURSDAY	FRIDAY
1	2 8-8:40 am 5th gr W	3 9-9:40 am 4th gr W	4 8-8:40 am 3d gr B	5
8	9 8-8:40 am 5th gr W	10 9-9:40 am 4th gr W	11 12-12:40 pm Kdg M	12 11:30-12 noon Special M
15	16 8-8:40 am 5th gr W	17 9-9:40 am 4th gr W	18 8-8:40 am 3d gr B	19
22	23 8-8:40 am 5th gr W 1:30-2:00 pm 2d gr M	24 9-9:40 am 4th gr W 12-12:40 pm 1st gr M	25 3-3:40 pm PreK M	26
29	30 8-8:30 am 5th gr W	31 9-9:40 am 4th gr W	Code for Planning: M = Monthly B = Biweekly W = Weekly	

In some schools a day is designated for planning. All teachers attend a cooperative planning session for their grade level during their contractual planning time on the specified day. Although scheduling all teachers on a particular day does not allow each teacher to select the most convenient time, library media specialists often make the idea more palatable by providing refreshments. The library media specialist is also able to spend the minutes between sessions pulling materials the teachers have requested or developing ideas for cooperative activities. Assistants can supervise sustained silent reading, show literature-related audiovisuals, or conduct other activities while the teachers are free for planning. Workdays or staff development days might be considered as cooperative planning days if other commitments, such as in-services or parent conferences, would not preclude such an arrangement. If grade level teams meet regularly, the library media specialist might attend some of their meetings. The library media specialist should maintain communication between infrequent sessions by sending notes.

The planning schedule may either be circulated at a staff meeting or circulated through the building for teachers and/or teams to indicate their preferred times. At the same time, the library media specialist may wish to distribute grade-level information skills scope and sequence for each grade level to the appropriate teachers. The teachers should be encouraged to review them and to keep them with their plan books for easy reference.

Certain teachers may choose to plan weekly while others plan every two weeks. It is suggested that planning be scheduled at least monthly for each grade level until the planning routine is established. If a routine planning time is not established, many teachers will not find the time to plan and students will suffer by not having media program experiences.

Once established, planning times may be changed, but these sessions are the only fixed part of the library media specialist's schedule. Instruction or other activities must never preempt this time. To ensure that other activities are not inadvertently scheduled for one of the session times, it is recommended that the library media specialist insert the planning times for the entire year in the plan book or on the schedule where instruction is recorded. Using a pencil will allow changes to be made as necessary.

PLANNING TEAMS

Planning may occur with individual teachers, all teachers at a particular grade level, or a multidisciplinary team. Ideally, a teacher planning individually with the library media specialist ensures that each activity is designed to meet the needs of the students in that particular class. Realistically, many elementary schools are so large that planning individually with each teacher would consume the majority of the library media specialist's working hours. Therefore, it is more feasible to plan with several teachers at a time. Obviously, the more teachers involved in the planning process the longer the decision making will take.

Planning may occur with all teachers for the grade level present or with only selected teachers. Divide the disciplines and select a teacher to represent all teachers of that grade level for planning in that particular subject area. For example, one of the fifth-grade teachers may develop lessons with the library media specialist correlated with the science curriculum, another will work on social studies, and another on reading. If grade-level planning occurs with a team representative, each teacher in that grade level should serve as the team representative at some point during the year.

Special area teachers, such as physical education, special education, art, music, and guidance may meet with the team or plan individually. When special area teachers share the responsibility for providing planning time through a rotation schedule, team planning encourages opportunities for relevant activities. Another configuration is that of the multidisciplinary team. Such a team has representation from each of the subject areas, each of the grade levels, and the specialists. The multidisciplinary team is most appropriate when planning school-wide activities or in those schools which choose a school-wide focus or theme each year. A multidisciplinary team may be formed to plan special activities as necessary, while all other planning occurs with individual teachers or grade levels. In many instances the library media advisory committee could serve as a multi-disciplinary team. If a multidisciplinary team is the primary means of cooperative planning, it is suggested that a rotation be established so that all teachers have the opportunity to share in the planning process.

PLANNING LOCATION

Planning may occur either in the library media center or in the classroom. Teachers tend to be more comfortable in their own territory; if they are not prepared for the session, they can have ready access to their curriculum and schedules. At times, planning can begin more promptly in the classroom than in the library media center. When planning takes place in the classroom, the library media specialist is able to observe classwork and bulletin boards. When planning occurs in the library media center, the teacher is able to see what is happening in the media program. Materials are accessible and more easily disseminated. It is probably advantageous to vary the location of the planning sessions.

PLANNING FORMS

Design planning instruments to collect the information appropriate for the planning team configuration and to be consistent with the goals and objectives of the media program.

Teachers can also provide a nine-week planning sheet to alert the library media specialist to possible future cooperative topics and units (see figure 4.3).

Teachers who have taught in isolation are often suspicious of the library media specialist who asks what is occurring in the classroom. Perhaps a form might make the questions less threatening. Distribute planning sheets to the appropriate teachers with a memo (see figure 4.4) attached explaining what to do with the sheet, why the sheet is used, and the date for return.

The planning sheet is the only form the teacher completes. It is not intended to duplicate the teacher's lesson plans, but rather to include only the information necessary to initiate cooperative planning. The planning sheet may be used to indicate monthly or grading period topics and should reflect the school's curriculum. A monthly planning sheet is preferable for allowing the teacher to be more specific, while coverage of the grading period allows longer-range planning. The form could also be used for an entire school year which would list annual units which are library-based. Figures 4.5 and 4.6 are sample filled-in planning sheets.

The planning sheet encourages efficient use of valuable planning time by allowing the library media specialist to gather materials prior to planning and to formulate suggestions for curriculum integration. The planning sheet may also be shared with other special area teachers to help them integrate their areas into the classroom curricula. When posted on an easily accessible, large curriculum calendar or compiled on a single sheet and distributed to the entire staff, the information from the planning sheet increases curriculum awareness and leads to the sharing of materials and resources.

(Text continues on page 66.)

Fig. 4.3. Planning Sheet.

Grade _____   Teacher _____   _____ Nine Weeks

Reading	Math
Social Studies	Language
Science	Special Projects/Events

Problem Areas or Skill Weaknesses:

Fig. 4.4. Planning sheet memo.

Teachers:

Please take a few minutes to complete the attached media planning sheet for the nine weeks indicated. You need only put general areas of study, but through this we will be able to make efficient use of our cooperative planning time and I will be prepared with ideas and materials. I will be sharing these sheets with the other special area teachers so that they too may plan cooperatively with you when appropriate.

Please indicate the approximate time frames for the various subject area topics as well as the dates for any special projects and return the sheet to the library media center by _____.

Thank you for your time and cooperation in helping us provide relevant learning experiences for our children.

Fig. 4.5. Planning Sheet.

Grade __5__   Teacher _Douglas/Durak_   __2nd__ Nine Weeks

Reading

BOOK CHECK

SS Rdg

Oral Lit: Thanksgiving
              Treasure
Witch of Blackbird Pond

Research for Oral Project

Reference: Thesaurus

Math

MEASUREMENT
  Balance Scales
  Metric Scale
  Meters/Liters/Grams
    (to the tenth)
GEO — ME — TREE UNIT
  Protractor/Compass/Ruler
  Constructions

Social Studies

What Columbus
Found:
  Continents/
    People
Newcomers to the Americas
Time Line: Explorers/
              Biographies?
European Colonies

English Colonies

Language

VERBS/OBJECTS/TENSES
PRONOUNS/CONTRACTIONS
DESCRIPTIVE PARAGRAPHS
  > Five Senses/Word Choices
  > Details/Describing Words
ORAL PRESENTATION

POETRY
  (Need Poetry Express)

Science

SOLAR SYSTEM
STARS/CONSTELLATIONS
MATTER: Physical Properties
          Chemical Properties

Five Senses/Word Choices
  Descriptive Words

Special Projects/Events

Planet/Constellation Project
  (Oral Presentation)
Raintree Contest
Fla. Poets' Contest
Island of Blue Dolphin:
                    film

Johnny Tremain: film

Problem Areas or Skill Weaknesses:

Fig. 4.6. Planning Sheet.

Grade __5__   Teacher *Lipscomb/Lehman*   *2nd* Nine Weeks

Reading	Math

References/Research:
  Encyclopedia
  Biographical Dictionary
  Nonfiction Books
  Atlases
  Table of Contents
  Index
Fiction: Author Studies
	Volume/Mass/Density
	Temperature
	- - - - - - - - - -
	Balance Scales
	Graduated Cylinders
	Thermometers
	Metric beakers/Liters

Social Studies	Language

The Thirteen Colonies
The Revolution
The New Nation
 	
Oral Lit:
  Witch of Blackbird Pond
 	
Geography of United States
	Dictionary/Reference Skills
	Punctuation Skills
	Word Choice: Five Senses
	   Describing Words
	↓ *Choices of Detail*
	Poetry Writing
	Report Writing: Topics
	      Outlines
	      Notetaking

Science	Special Projects/Events

Matter:
Physical + chemical properties
Atoms/Molecules/Elements
Process Skill Labs:
  Observation
  Recording/Communicating
  Measuring/Describing
Sources of Energy
Health: Transport Systems
	Poetry Groups: Sensory Description
	    of Objects
	Timeline Project: Explorers
	Biopoem Project: Great American
	    Individual in History
	State Project: Outline
	      Notes
	      Booklet
	Field Trip: John Young
	      Planetarium
	  Loch Haven Art Museum

Problem Areas or Skill Weaknesses:

The use of planning sheets does not preclude spontaneity (see "A Case in Point," p. 74). The benefits of the flexible access program must include spur-of-the-moment activities and filling immediate needs. Expect the unexpected and remain positive. Major requests not calendared should be the exception rather than the rule, but the library media center should be flexible and adaptable—like an emergency room—even accommodating last-moment requests.

LIBRARY MEDIA SPECIALIST RESPONSIBILITIES

Preparing for Planning Sessions

The library media specialist must be prepared for each planning session. Use a planning notebook to keep all materials readily accessible. The notebook can be organized by grade or by teachers and might include:

1. *Grade appropriate scope and sequence of information skills* (see figure 4.7). The skills for each grade are extracted from the total information skills scope and sequence. The skills checklist includes all skills appropriate for a particular grade level, teachers' names, and spaces to indicate the date each skill is taught to each class. The library media specialist can tell at a glance which skills have been covered. Details of a particular lesson can be traced quickly in the plan book. Using the checklist, the teacher and the library media specialist can determine which skills may need greater emphasis. Additional skills listed can then be considered for inclusion as the school's scope and sequence statement is updated.

2. *Completed and blank planning sheets.* The completed planning sheets can also be used as notetaking sheets. The library media specialist can indicate suggested integrated activities on the sheet prior to the planning session and mark with asterisks the units for which teachers would like materials gathered.

3. *Scheduling forms.* After determining the frequency of the lessons for the activities planned, you may wish to actually schedule specific times by using a form, rather than have all teachers wait as you schedule them one by one. You may have the teachers indicate two preferences on a simple form (see figure 4.8) and notify them of the specific times you were able to schedule them for the cooperatively planned lessons.

4. *Plans of previous lessons* (see figures 4.9 and 4.10). Invariably a teacher asks to schedule a lesson or unit "like we did last year." File previous lessons in the notebook so you don't have to recreate the plans.

(Text continues on page 71.)

Fig. 4.7. Scope and Sequence for Elementary Media Skills: Second Grade.

Teacher Name (one per column); Dates Taught in Box.

I. PARTS OF A BOOK					
A. Index					
B. Glossary					
C. Dedication					
II. LOCATION AND ARRANGE-MENT OF PRINT MATERIALS					
A. Fiction					
B. Nonfiction					
C. Magazines					
D. Newspapers					
III. PUBLIC CATALOG					
A. Arrangement of Cards or Screen					
1. Alphabetical					
B. Alphabetical Guides or Querying for Success					
IV. REFERENCE SKILLS					
A. Alphabetizing					
1. To third letter					
B. Glossary					
V. REFERENCE TOOLS					
A. Encyclopedias					
1. Topical					
B. Nonfiction					
VI. MEDIA PRODUCTION					
A. Audiotape					
B. Posters					
VII. INFORMATION THINKING					
A. Accuracy					
B. Preference					
ADDITIONAL SKILLS					

Fig. 4.8. Preferred Library Media Times.

Unit/Lesson/Activity _____ Teacher _____
    Entire class _____
    Small group _____
    Individuals _____

1st Choice(s) _____

2nd Choice(s) _____

Comments: _____

_____

_____

_____

_____

_____

_____

_____

Fig. 4.9. Library Media Center Unit Planning Form.

Unit Title: _____

Teacher _____ Group _____

Scheduled for _____ Location _____

Objectives: _____

_____

_____

_____

Skills: _____

_____

_____

Media: _____

_____

_____

Activities: _____

_____

_____

End Product: _____

Responsibilities: _____

_____

_____

_____

_____

Evaluation: _____

_____

_____

_____

Comments/Suggestions: _____

_____

_____

Fig. 4.10. Library Media Center Unit Planning Form.

Unit Title: *Africa*

Teacher *Jamison*   Group *3rd grade*

Scheduled for *Jan. 27th, 10:45-11:30*   Location *LMC*

Objectives: *The student will be able to define folktale. The student will be able to locate a folktale for a classroom assignment. The student will be able to discuss "A Story, A Story" as a folktale.*

Skills: *III. G. Folktale*
    VIII. C. Location and Arrangement of Nonfiction

Media: *"A Story, A Story" by Gail Haley, Anansi stories*

Activities: *Cooking chocolate spiders while sharing Anansi stories; Stinger Starter 6*

End Product: *Chocolate spiders*

Responsibilities: *Teacher/LMS team cooking chocolate spiders and Stinger Starters. LMS to do folktales in prep. for other special teacher projects. Introduce the author to the students so they recognize all of her work.*

Evaluation: *Heightened awareness—students still bring in materials to classroom and mention Africa although unit is over. Retention of folktale characteristics has been excellent.*

Comments/Suggestions: *Use modified chocolate spider recipe and schedule or allow time to harden (at least 15 extra minutes)*

The library media specialist must consider the personalities involved in the planning team and the communication patterns that have already been established with the teachers. Conflict is inevitable in the planning process. It arises from scarce resources, unmet expectations, unclear or different goals, lack of role clarity, lack of information, misinformation, and different methods and/or styles. Careful preparation for the planning process helps prevent many sources of conflict. Anticipate possible objections or conflicts by having a colleague play devil's advocate and ask questions that might arise.[1] Anticipate which teachers may have objections and talk to them prior to the planning session.

The smaller and more homogeneous the group, the easier it is to reach a decision. For larger and more diverse teams, prepare an agenda or a memo to distribute to all team members so that everyone has the same focus during the meeting (see figure 4.11). Place items requiring immediate decisions at the top of the agenda. Schedule open-ended discussions at the end. To promote faster decision making, state the agenda items succinctly but specifically. Use a statement such as "Decide between individual class or grade level storytimes" rather than "Discuss storytimes."

Estimate the time it will take to discuss each item and indicate that time next to the item on the agenda. Refer to the estimated time if necessary to end a discussion. If time constraints do not permit announcements to be made, circulate a memo for routine information that does not require discussion.[2] Copy the agenda on the reverse of the appropriate planning sheet to keep all notes concerning that planning session on a single sheet.

Fig. 4.11. Cooperative Planning Session Agenda.

Team _____   Date _____

ITEMS TO BE DISCUSSED:

ANNOUNCEMENTS:

COMMENTS:

REMINDERS:

Scheduled time _____

Actual time _____

Prior to each planning session, compile suggestions for relevant activities (see "Additional Readings," pages 79-81 for activity ideas). When developing program ideas, consider:

1. *Your personal interests.* Cultivate ideas you will enjoy developing. Concentrate on activities that interest you and that you feel comfortable with. Ignore other activities or suggest that teachers on the planning team incorporate them in the classroom.

   The inspiration for a library media activity might come from a favorite story. For a class enjoying stories about mice, share Jane Numeroff's *If You Give a Mouse a Cookie* (Harper, 1985) and follow the reading with a sequencing activity in which the children, holding actual objects or pictures of objects from the story, arrange themselves in the order of those items' appearance in the story.

2. *Successful lessons you have done in the past.* In my pre-flexible access days I was in the midst of sharing a picture book with fourth graders one afternoon when the principal, the assistant principal, and approximately 150 fifth graders entered the library media center, each carrying a chair. The library media center also served as the auditorium; to my surprise they had come to arrange chairs for the parent-teacher meeting scheduled for that evening. As we became increasingly surrounded by chairs, the eyes of my thirty students stayed riveted to the book. After the children had returned to their classroom the assistant principal approached me, asking "What in the world were you reading? They didn't even notice us!" It was Gail Haley's *A Story, A Story* (Atheneum, 1970). You can be assured that this is the book I always use to introduce folktales. I sometimes even arrange to teach that lesson when I know I will be observed or evaluated! Revamp a lesson you enjoy doing to correlate with the basal text or with another area of the curriculum.

3. *Something you have always wanted to try.* You may create your own correlations for the basal, a new school-wide program, or the comprehensive plans. These correlations may be isolated lessons, centers or units that extend over several weeks, or celebrations for each grade or the entire school. If you prefer, use commercial sources of curriculum-integrated media skills activity ideas (see appendix E). Each textbook teacher's edition includes supplementary activities from which you can choose an appropriate activity that the teacher will not be using. Teacher's editions not only provide specific relevant ideas but also can serve as a springboard for your cooperatively planned units.

4. *Your areas of expertise.* If one of your strengths is equipment utilization, plan activities based on audiovisual resources.

5. *Experiences you think all children should have*. You may wish to develop oral literature units or pursue other phases of cultural literacy.

6. *New ways of using resources*. "New" materials recently discovered on the shelf can provide the catalyst for an activity. When browsing through *Arthur's Valentine* by Marc Brown (Little Brown, 1980), I discovered that the story would be perfect for the staff to dramatize for the students as part of our Holiday Happening. We ended the story by treating each student with one of Arthur's kind of kisses, a Hershey's Kiss. That and watching Francine (a teacher) pucker up for a kiss from Arthur (the assistant principal) ensured an experience that the students did not soon forget.

During Planning

Set the tone. If you want the teachers to be prompt and use planning time efficiently, be prepared and direct the meeting accordingly. Let them know you are ready:

1. Have sufficient seating arranged prior to their arrival.

2. Start promptly.

3. Do not wait for latecomers.

The effective planning session leader (1) reads nonverbal behavior, (2) involves all teachers in the discussion, and (3) draws on the strengths of the group. Invite teachers to participate by saying that you have certain ideas about a particular topic but are not sure how to implement them.

Every teacher is good at some important aspect of the planning process. Watch for the participant who shows particular interest in the topic being discussed and ask that person to follow up on that project. Until recently I generally relied on the team leaders for each grade to assume the responsibilities related to a unit planned for that grade. During an initial planning session for a unit, one of the teachers who often had very little to say was making numerous suggestions. I realized that I had been doing as principals often do, "rewarding" the competence of the proven leaders with more work. I decided to capitalize on this teacher's enthusiasm and communicated further plans and questions about the unit to the team through her. She assumed ownership of the unit and prepared the materials. Since then I have made a point of identifying the team member who appears most interested in each unit and relying on that person to provide the leadership.

In managing the planning session, the well-organized library media specialist is conscious of time, adheres to the agenda, and makes sure action is taken, responsibilities are delegated, and deadlines set. Conclude the meeting with a summary of the decisions that were made. Reinforcing the teachers' sense of accomplishment will make them more eager to attend the next planning session.

After Planning

Circulate some type of follow-up memo after the planning session. The memo should include what was discussed during planning and when the implementation of the activities will occur. Write the memo specifically for each time or use the form in figure 4.9. Give a copy of the form to the appropriate teachers to include in their plan books. File a copy in the planning notebook for future use.

A Case in Point

Even though one might have the unit planning process thoroughly organized, locking into one system for years can actually retard the flexibility of the program. For example, the long-range planning forms presume that teachers teach in discreet curricular areas that do not overlap. Thus a resource-based teaching unit is social studies based, science based, or literature based.

In the past few years, many teachers have adopted an integrated approach to teaching where many of the traditional disciplines are meshed under an umbrella theme. For example, a theme of monsters might be the topic under which literature, letter writing, communities, transportation, measurement, geometry, and multiplication are taught. In this case, the planning forms traditionally used may not respond to immediate needs and would have to be redesigned. Figure 4.12 is a blank form I used recently with second-grade teachers to plan an integrated unit about monsters. The teachers and I then filled in both content and information skills activities as appropriate to create a *whole* or *theme* study.

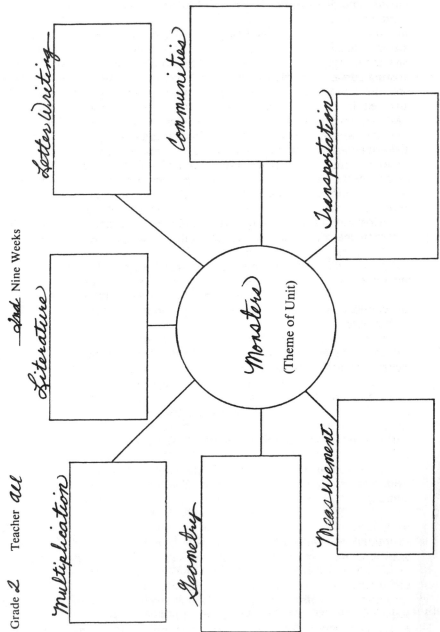

Fig. 4.12. Thematic Planning Sheet.

Grade *2*   Teacher *all*   *2nd* Nine Weeks

TEACHER RESPONSIBILITIES

Before Planning

The role of the teacher in the planning process may be that of content specialist. The teacher often provides the subject expertise while the library media specialist functions as the information and resource specialist. However, since both the teacher and the library media specialist may be equally knowledgeable about content and information skills they will make contributions in both areas to the planning experience. For the most productive use of planning sessions, the teacher should:

1. Be familiar with the information skills at the grade level by having reviewed the appropriate scope and sequence.

2. Review the completed planning sheet and make notes of relevant points to discuss.

3. Be prepared with ideas for cooperative library media experiences.

4. Be prepared with well-thought-out ideas for developing assignments utilizing media.

The teacher is responsible for attending the cooperative planning sessions at the time and day previously designated. The teacher should bring a plan book and any relevant curriculum guides or textbooks.

During Planning

When one initiates cooperative planning, the process should be the primary focus, the product secondary. As both the teachers and the library media specialist become more comfortable with the planning process, the product will become primary. Together the library media specialist and the teacher can plan:

- a repertoire of units for two-person teaching,

- units that all teachers in the group can use, and

- units for in-depth study in a grade level or school-wide.

Ideally, all instructional activities are initiated through cooperative planning with input from teachers and the library media specialist. However, in practice cooperation is not always possible because there is one library media specialist serving a number of teachers. There are times, for example when creating reading stimulation activities, that the library media specialist may plan an experience and then inform teachers of the availability of the lesson. Teachers then determine if and when to bring the class. Flexible access library media programs provide the best of both worlds: teacher-initiated and library media specialist-initiated experiences.

The planning session provides time to determine who will do what, when it will be done, how it will be done, and how it will be measured and evaluated (see figures 4.1 and 4.9). For each lesson or unit a determination is made about:

1. *Objectives*. The "what" of a particular lesson or unit should be specific, attainable, and quantifiable. At this point it is often necessary to clarify terminology.

2. *Skills*. Information skills are most effectively taught when integrated into the curriculum rather than taught in isolation. Enumerate these skills, concepts, and attitudes at this point in the planning process. Referring to the scope and sequence checklist (figure 4.7) will assist in determining those grade-appropriate skills which may be introduced, reinforced, or extended.

3. *Media*. Select specific resources and discuss the usage sequence and patterns. Designate the media as appropriate for large-group or center activities, for media center or classroom use. Identify commercially produced materials for use or design and plan locally produced media to meet the special needs of the lesson.

4. *Activities*. Determine the method of introducing the unit, relating the activities to classroom experiences, stimulating interest, and maintaining interest in the unit. The library media specialist or teacher may employ a storytime for introducing the unit, a demonstration to stimulate interest, and a display to maintain interest.

5. *Grouping*. Who will be instructed? Will the entire class participate in the activities or only special groups or individuals? Grouping may be done on the basis of needs, interests, abilities, the amount of materials, or the teaching strategies used. The classroom teacher may have sufficient information from previous experiences for making this decision, or it may be necessary to devise a prelearning activity to identify the specific students to be instructed. Introduce some projects to the entire class, then schedule small groups for follow-up activities in the media center.

6. *End Product*. Loertscher provides a checklist of types of teaching activities and one of end products.[3] These are extremely useful in planning varied experiences. Add these to your planning notebook for ready reference.

7. *Responsibilities*. Presenting the lesson is the responsibility of both the library media specialist and the teacher. Some activities will be conducted by the teacher alone, others jointly, and still others by the library media specialist alone.

   Because activities do not always go according to plan, it is necessary to determine how the project will be completed if sufficient time has not been allotted. Additional time may be scheduled as necessary, the time for the concluding lesson may be routinely extended to allow time for each student to complete the activity, or the project may be completed in the classroom under the direction of the teacher.

If there is work to be graded or checked, also determine whether the work will be checked by the library media specialist or the teacher.

8. *Evaluation*. Determine the means for evaluating each lesson during the planning process. The evaluation may be informal, such as observation, or formal, such as a test or an additional application activity. Although the means of evaluation and the time it will occur are decided during the cooperative planning session, informal evaluation should occur continuously throughout the teaching/learning process, with necessary changes made during the process.

The formal evaluation of the unit as a whole should occur at the first planning session after the conclusion of the unit. The planning team will want to identify:

- experiences that were successful and should be continued,

- experiences that were unsuccessful and should be deleted or modified,

- changes that should be made the next time the unit is taught,

- components of the present unit that could be integrated into future units, and

- materials for purchase.

CONCLUSION

The amount of time spent in completing the "Library Media Center Unit Planning Form" (figure 4.9) and in participating in cooperative planning sessions is more than repaid by the relevant experiences planned for students and the professional growth experienced by teachers and the library media specialist. Without thorough planning, resource-based instruction is more likely to fail.

PROFESSIONAL ACTIVITIES

1. Determine the planning team composition that would be most effective in your school.

2. Design cooperative planning tools to be used in your flexible access library media program.

3. Schedule a planning session with a team. Teach the cooperatively planned lesson format.

NOTES

[1]"Master Teacher Tips: Staff Relationships," *The Master Teacher* 17 (March 1986): 4.

[2]Julie Bailey, "The Fine Art of Leading a Meeting," *Working Woman* (August 1987): 68-70, 103.

[3]David V. Loertscher, *Taxonomies of the School Library Media Program* (Englewood, Colo.: Libraries Unlimited, 1988).

ADDITIONAL READINGS

Berkowitz, Bob, and Joyce Berkowitz. "Thinking Is Critical: Moving Students beyond Location." *School Library Media Activities Monthly* 3 (May 1987): 25-27, 50.
    These authors provide directions for and examples of "information analysis sheets," which require students to use higher-level thinking skills.

Brown, David M. "A Half-Time Compromise to the Whole Language Approach." In *School Library Media Annual*, edited by Jane Bandy Smith, 6: 36-42. Littleton, Colo.: Libraries Unlimited, 1988.
    Provides suggestions for the library media specialist to become actively involved with the "whole reader" approach. Additional sources for reading, listening, and viewing activities are noted.

Cullinan, Bernice E., ed. *Children's Literature in the Reading Program*. Newark, Del.: International Reading Association, 1987.
    A practical compilation of a wide variety of articles on reading in the elementary school. Boxes containing teaching ideas are interspersed throughout, making it quick to peruse for suggestions. The foreword by Tomie dePaola is of special interest to library media specialists advocating access to materials.

Eisenberg, Michael. "Curriculum Mapping and Implementation of an Elementary School Media Skills Curriculum." *School Library Media Quarterly* (Fall 1984): 411-18.

Harsh, Ann. "Teach Mathematics with Children's Literature." *Young Children* 42 (Summer 1987): 24-29.
    Specific titles are suggested that introduce pre-number concepts to young children.

Hart, Thomas L. *Instruction in School Library Media Center Use (K-12)*. 2d ed. Chicago: American Library Association, 1985.
    This edition presents numerous examples of library media activities arranged by both grade level and skill, as well as reprints of articles on teaching library media skills.

Haycock, Ken. "Hard Times ... Hard Choices." *Emergency Librarian* 9 (May/
June 1982): 5.
This editorial emphasizes the importance of flexible scheduling to facilitate
cooperative planning and teaching by library media specialist and teacher.

Hurst, Carol Otis, and Leslie Witherell. "Seeing History." *Early Years* (October
1986): 43-51.
Suggests picture book titles set from the 1700s to the 1980s to teach
American history to elementary age students. Activities are included for each
title.

Irving, Jan, and Robin Currie. *Full Speed Ahead: Stories and Activities for
Children on Transportation*. Englewood, Colo.: Libraries Unlimited, 1988.
Original stories, fingerplays, skits, and 125 picturebook titles focusing on
eight modes of transportation are presented in this activity book. The skills index,
though emphasizing readiness skills, is useful for locating relevant primary
information skills.

Irving, Jan, and Robin Currie. *Glad Rags: Stories and Activities Featuring
Clothes for Children*. Englewood, Colo.: Libraries Unlimited, 1987.
Hats, shoes, and all kinds of apparel are the focus of this activity book for
primary students.

Irving, Jan, and Robin Currie. *Mudluscious: Stories and Activities Featuring
Food for Preschool Children*. Littleton, Colo.: Libraries Unlimited, 1986.
Numerous suggestions are offered for integrating skills through every
imaginable activity relating to food. The activities are appropriate for primary
students.

Jay, M. Ellen. "The Elementary School Library Media Teacher's Role in Educating Students to Think: Suggested Activities for Fostering the Development of Thinking Skills." *School Library Media Quarterly* (Fall 1986):
28-32.
Jay describes specific critical thinking activities appropriate for the library
media specialist to use with primary age children.

Leonard, Phyllis B. *Choose, Use, Enjoy, Share: Library Media Skills for the
Gifted Child*. Littleton, Colo.: Libraries Unlimited, 1985.
One in a series of books on teaching library media skills, this volume
suggests methods for introducing resources and skills to correlated assignments
for the elementary age gifted child.

O'Brien, Kathy, and Darlene K. Stoner. "Increasing Environmental Awareness through Children's Literature." *The Reading Teacher* 41 (October
1987): 14-19.

Paulin, Mary Ann. *Creative Uses of Children's Literature*. Hamden, Conn.: Library Professional Publications, 1982.
Over 700 pages packed with ways to extend children's books. The extensive subject index is extremely useful for selecting titles related to specific topics.

Seaver, Alice R. *Library Media Skills: Strategies for Instructing Primary Students*. Littleton, Colo.: Libraries Unlimited, 1984.
Suggestions are given for planning cooperatively with classroom teachers to provide library media activities for students in grades K to three.

Smith, Adele C. "The Library Media Specialist's Role in Promoting Critical Thinking Skills." In *School Library Media Annual*, edited by Shirley L. Aaron and Pat Scales, 4: 286-96. Littleton, Colo.: Libraries Unlimited, 1986.
Smith details ways to integrate the reading of quality children's literature, content-area requirements, and various levels of assignments in cooperatively planned lessons.

Turner, Philip M. *Helping Teachers Teach*. Littleton, Colo.: Libraries Unlimited, 1985.

Turner, Philip M., ed. *A Casebook for "Helping Teachers Teach."* Englewood, Colo.: Libraries Unlimited, 1988.
Thirteen case studies illustrate library media specialists at each level helping teachers create, implement, and evaluate instructional units.

"Units and Unit Planning for Library Media Skills Instruction." *School Library Media Activities Monthly* 3 (October 1986): 32-33.
This short article identifies and defines unit components and includes a planning chart useful when designing units.

Walker, Tom. "Demystifying Planning." *School Library Media Activities Monthly* 2 (September 1985): 44.

Wallingford, Carol. "School Library Media Services to Kindergarten Students." In *School Library Media Annual*, edited by Shirley L. Aaron and Pat Scales, 4: 260-76. Littleton, Colo.: Libraries Unlimited, 1986.
Examples of activities cooperatively planned by the library media specialist and kindergarten teacher are shared as well as kindergarten information skills taught in various states.

Zlotnick, Barbara Bradley. *Ready for Reference: Media Skills for Intermediate Students*. Littleton, Colo.: Libraries Unlimited, 1984.
This book describes the role of the library media specialist and of the teacher in cooperative planning and presents a variety of skills and strategies for integrating lessons in diverse areas of the curriculum.

Chapter 5
Implementing Your Flexible Access Program

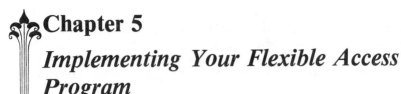

This chapter provides information to assist the library media specialist in:

1. *visualizing how an entire program might be put into action,*

2. *accomplishing the transition from planning to implementing a flexible access library media program,*

3. *selecting the central focus of the program, and*

4. *monitoring and maintaining a flexible access library media program.*

A successful flexible access library media program takes time: time to grow, time to correct mistakes, and time for continued planning and improvement. To accomplish all the steps discussed in this book will take months, even years. This chapter assumes that a great deal of time has already been spent in planning for, gaining acceptance for, and planning with teachers for resource-based units of instruction. And so you begin. The first part of this chapter discusses the responsibilities of each crucial group or person affected by flexible access: the principal, the teachers, the students, and the library media assistant. Each will have a role to perform if the entire program is going to succeed.

THE ROLE OF THE PRINCIPAL

The principal articulates the vision of the school to the staff. The principal who is committed to a flexible access library media program communicates the role of the library media program in that vision. During the initial stages of implementation, the principal talks to the staff in detail about the role of the flexible access library media program. The principal continues to be responsible for making teachers aware of the expectations of and for the program. This vision is shared during interviews with prospective staff, during parent meetings, in conversations, in newsletters, and in memos to the faculty.

When interviewing new teachers, the principal who is dedicated to the flexible access library media program concept asks them about their experiences with a flexible program and their willingness to participate in cooperative planning. "How have you made use of library media resources in your teaching?" "How have you worked with a library media specialist?" If a teacher's style of teaching is textbook oriented, the principal will want to consider whether that person will enhance the philosophy of the school.

To implement a flexible access library media program, the principal has already pledged that the use of the library media center will be flexibly structured and time will be allowed for planning and curriculum work. The principal must continue to provide a safe environment for implementing the program. Mistakes will be made, but the teachers and the library media specialist should not fear failure. The principal must be willing to share the failures and the accolades, rather than blame the library media specialist or teachers and abandon the program at the first sign of difficulties. The teachers will continue to experiment with ideas if they realize that the principal will not seek to assign blame but rather wants to work with them to find out what happened and what can be learned from the experience.

The principal should be aware that what may have been the quiet inner sanctum of the library is now sometimes a bustling center of activity and at other times a quiet place. During my first year with a flexible access program, the principal would walk through the library media center and there would not be a child in sight. I would be busy with a myriad of other responsibilities of the program, but where were the children of all age levels participating in simultaneous activities? They were in the classroom waiting to descend on the media center the moment the principal stepped into his office. When this happened I would immediately ask the principal to come back.

The simultaneous activity of circulation, research, and instruction obviously does increase noise and movement in the library media center. When a flexible access library media program is implemented, a library media center that was previously used once a week for a set amount of time may no longer look neat and orderly. When viewing my new library media center, a colleague of mine remarked, "I can tell this is your library media center. It has just the right amount of disarray." With the continuous and simultaneous activity of a flexible access program, having the shelves in perfect order and the tables cleared and neat will be almost impossible. A flexible access program is not an excuse to become disorderly, but it is inevitable that the library media center when *being* used will certainly *look* used.

The principal's commitment to a flexible access library media program is further reflected in the budget. The principal should seek ways to provide the resources and personnel necessary for a successful program. As mentioned previously, the resources necessary for program implementation usually already exist within the building. Often what is needed is to reassess resources and use them in creative, innovative ways.

To ensure successful implementation of the program, the principal also must support in-service activities that demonstrate the use of information resources and technology for small-group, individual, and class projects and encourage teachers to allow students increased access to the library media center. The supportive principal is a model of the behavior desired of students and staff. In our school, the closed circuit television system has allowed opportunities for the principal to share books with the children. The titles included in the list of the children's favorite book award program in our state have been read during live broadcasts from the principal's office and in the media center. The principal should be an active participant in the program, dramatizing books or reading aloud to students and staff, using the library media center for research or for pleasure reading, and providing time for the entire school to read. The principal who enters the library media center to read or use reference sources soon is surrounded by students following that example.

A once-reluctant principal was transformed into an eager entertainer after giving one Literacy Day performance of Irma Black's *The Little Old Man Who Could Not Read* (Whitman, 1968) to primary students. Another principal rearranged his schedule to be able to be the lead performer in a rendition of Nuntean's *The Old Man and the Afternoon Cat* (Parents Magazine Press, 1982) for Children's Book Week.

Many schools designate a time for sustained silent reading when everyone in the school spends the allotted time enjoying a book or other reading material. Whatever title is used for the program, DEAR (Drop Everything and Read), SQUIRT (Sustained Quiet Uninterrupted Individual Reading Time) or SSR (Sustained Silent Reading), the principal who encourages such a time reinforces the value that is placed on reading and on the accessibility of materials. Continuous involvement in the library media program will enable the principal to explain the flexible access program to parents, community, and school board.

The active principal will take frequent opportunities to provide recognition to the library media specialist and staff members. A note indicating that a teacher's efforts in planning are appreciated or attendance at a cooperatively planned activity will encourage continued teacher participation in the flexible access library media program. Positive comments made to staff inspire them to make the entire school an extension of the library media center. The principal will also need to take time to participate in and discuss the program evaluation and respond to any flexible access reports which may be generated.

THE ROLE OF THE TEACHERS

Teachers who find themselves in the midst of a changing support system are most successful when they expect some successes, some failures, and certainly some inconvenience. Those who withhold judgment on initial attempts are in the best position to work out a system that will be in their own best interest.

One of the key factors in resource-based instruction is to be flexible. By coupling flexibility with a keen sense of analysis of what techniques are most successful with students, teachers and library media specialists can experiment, accept; experiment, reject; experiment, revise, and try again. Teachers who enjoy variety in their teaching strategies are likely to succeed first. Those who have more rigid teaching styles will experience more frustration and possible rejection.

THE ROLE OF THE STUDENTS

The goal of the flexible access library media program should be conveyed continuously to the students. Provide students with numerous opportunities to show when that goal is being achieved. The classroom teacher prepares students by making them aware of the purpose for their visits, whether as a large group or individually. Students are aware of the high expectations for their behavior and performance in the library media center. In our school, we are not often disappointed. When treated with respect and made aware of the high standards set for them, students respond accordingly. They respond accordingly also when treated with little respect and low expectations.

How can the library media specialist convey high expectations and respect to the students?

1. *Explain what you expect*. We expect that students will behave whether they are in a large group, a small group, or alone and whether they are working with the media staff, teachers, or volunteers.

2. *Explain the behavior rules*. Remember to have as few rules as possible. Elementary students tend to forget anything beyond four rules. Post the rules to remind students and inform others of expected behavior. Our rules are:

   a. Work so that your voice cannot be heard.

   b. Stay on task.

   c. Return materials after use.

3. *Explain the consequences of misbehavior*. Students who are working independently in our media center receive one warning. If another reminder is necessary they are sent back to the classroom. The teachers are aware that students who return from an activity before the scheduled time are being sent back for inappropriate behavior. It is necessary to send a note if they return early for an unrelated reason. The consequence for misbehavior when the entire class is in the library media center depends on the rules that have been established in each individual classroom.

4. *Enforce the rules*. Make students aware that when they choose to misbehave they will suffer the consequences. Have students identify their own inappropriate behavior.

5. *Provide positive reinforcement*. Let the students know when they are behaving as you expect. Tell them specifically what you notice about their behavior. "I like how quiet it is in the media center now. You are all busy working at your centers and I can't hear your voices."

Student Responsibilities

For the successful implementation of the flexible access library media program students also must assume responsibilities. To those unfamiliar with a flexible access library media program, the program may appear confusing and seem to be a waste of time; numerous students will be moving about, talking, and doing a variety of things. Students are responsible for knowing what they are supposed to be doing and then for doing it.

Students may be asked to:

1. sign-in so that attendance records may be kept (see figure 7.1 on page 111),

2. assist in planning activities,

3. assist in preparing activities/materials,

4. select materials,

5. evaluate materials, or

6. evaluate the library media program (see figure 7.4 on page 118).

Only by involving students, not just teaching them, can the program reach its full potential. The library media specialist is responsible for the continuous education of the students. Program information may be effectively disseminated to students through bookmark enclosures, with report cards, or by commenting on and signing work done in the media center. New student orientation might be provided through a welcomers club, audiovisual presentations, or pathfinder activities.

THE ROLE OF THE LIBRARY MEDIA ASSISTANT

The library media assistant plays a vital role in the successful implementation of a flexible access library media program. As a member of the library media staff this person must be educated about all aspects of the program and support the flexible access concept. It is not sufficient for the library media specialist alone to reflect this philosophy; all library media personnel must do so.

The library media assistant's schedule, like the specialist's, is flexible. Lunch and breaks vary from day to day based on the activities occurring in the media center. Routine tasks include shelving, typing, book repairs, processing materials, and any other jobs that contribute to a well-functioning library media center. By assuming responsibility for the preparation of instructional materials, supervision of materials circulation, and equipment maintenance, the library media assistant frees the library media specialist for professional program responsibilities.

MOVING TOWARD A FLEXIBLE ACCESS PROGRAM

Even though you may not be able to begin full implementation of a flexible access program, if you have considered the components of the program, you are ready to take the first step away from a rigid access schedule.

Scheduling

1. Ask that each grade schedule a cooperative planning time either before or after school or select one day of the week to plan with all grades during their planning time. If you currently provide planning time for teachers, request a substitute to cover your or the teacher's classes while you plan. If this is not feasible, plan an activity with the students that parents could help supervise while you meet with the teachers. A third possibility is having two classes take part in some activity in the library media center. Have one teacher supervise students while the other teacher plans with you. During the following week, the teachers reverse places.

2. If classes are currently scheduled in the media center on a regular basis, use the scheduled time for circulation and schedule instruction separately. If contractual planning time is not afforded by the library media specialist, teachers may supervise checkout. If the library media specialist provides contractual planning time, the library media assistant may supervise or you may implement a system for students to check out independently with a minimum of supervision.

Curriculum-Integrated Instruction

Since the objective of flexible access is to move closer to the center of the curriculum, that move must begin immediately. A few preliminaries might include:

1. Decide what should be taught at each particular grade level. Prepare a rough outline of skills you wish the students to acquire based on the information skills scope and sequence. The presence of a skill on the list does not mean that you must teach it. Include only those skills relevant to your particular situation.

2. Give each teacher a skills outline and a calendar with the special library media center-initiated emphases throughout the year, for example, School Library Media Week, Children's Book Week, reading stimulation programs, etc.

3. Distribute a long-range media planner to the faculty and ask that teachers complete one for each particular grade or class.

4. Decide if you want the focus to be school-wide, by grade level, or by individual class. It is recommended that for maximum visibility, activities in which the entire school or a grade level can participate be the focus of your energies during the initial implementation of your program. The amount of planning and preparation time it takes to provide library media experiences for individual classes, to say nothing of the instructional time, even in a moderate-sized school, is overwhelming. Concentrating on school-wide and grade level activities

during the first few months allows you to implement gradually those truly individualized media experiences.

Find a theme or an activity that a number of classes are doing. Some schools select a school-wide theme each month while others participate in state reading programs. Either would be an excellent focus for cooperative planning. Students and staff anticipate seasonal and grade level culminating activities and begin asking early in the year when they can expect certain events to occur. A reminder: Agree to do those things you enjoy. Chances are you will be asked to repeat them every year!

5. Review the long-range planner to determine library media activity priorities in relation to the school-wide or grade level focus. Develop a timeline showing anticipated cooperatively planned experiences.

6. Plan a few outstanding experiences rather than numerous mediocre activities. Once annual activities are calendared, activities for individual classes, small groups, or individual students can then be interspersed throughout the year.

THE CENTRAL AND ONGOING PROGRAM

If visitors were to examine a flexible library media center program, they would find that there are really two major components of action in a typical school day. First, there is the ongoing program. This component consists of many activities occurring simultaneously. Some of these activities are teacher-supervised, some are supervised by the library media assistant (or, peripherally, by the library media specialist if there is no aide), and others are self-supervised by the students (see figure 5.1). Children and teachers stream in and out of the center all day long engaging in activities that contribute to self-enjoyment, self-education, and curricular study. The number and types of these activities are a function of space, materials, teacher flexibility, and individual student interest. Children are taught to be independent users of the center and know what, when, where, and how they may participate in center activities. The library media center staff spends time creating activity possibilities and teaching the students and faculty how to maximize the center for personal or small- or large-group use with a minimum of attention from the library media center staff and with minimum distraction to the central program of the center (which requires most attention from the staff).

The second major component a visitor might see is the central program. The library media specialist spends a great deal of time thinking about, planning, and creating special resource-based teaching activities that have the most potential for a direct impact on the curriculum of the school. This program consists of three major types of resource-based teaching activities, which may all be happening simultaneously: school-wide theme activities, grade level theme activities, and individual units of instruction. A few examples of these major activities are included in the next section.

Fig. 5.1. Components of Flexible Access.

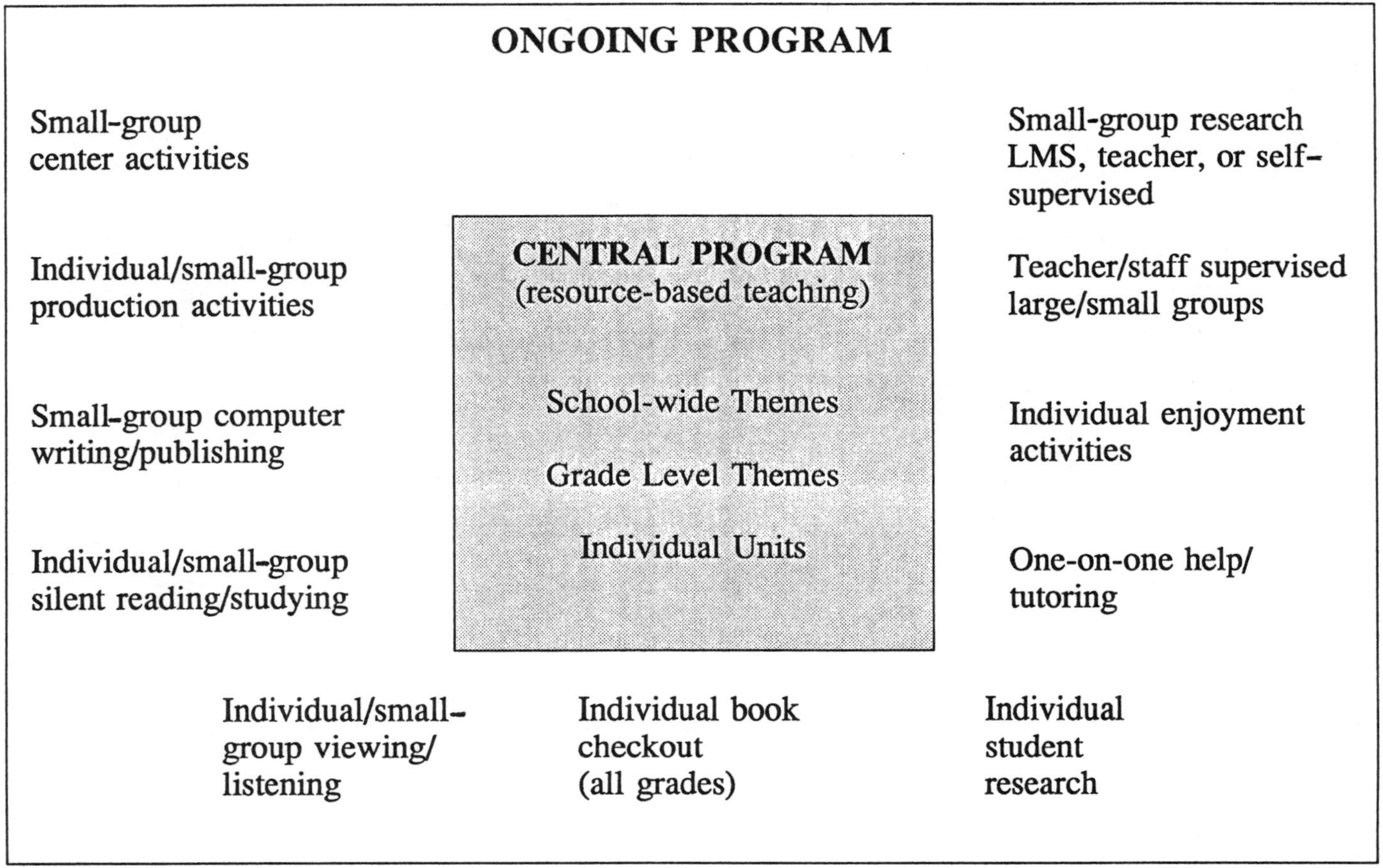

ONGOING PROGRAM

Small-group
center activities

Individual/small-group
production activities

Small-group computer
writing/publishing

Individual/small-group
silent reading/studying

Individual/small-
group viewing/
listening

Small-group research
LMS, teacher, or self-
supervised

Teacher/staff supervised
large/small groups

Individual enjoyment
activities

One-on-one help/
tutoring

Individual
student
research

CENTRAL PROGRAM
(resource-based teaching)

School-wide Themes

Grade Level Themes

Individual Units

Individual book
checkout
(all grades)

Creativity, close planning with teachers, and the unbridled energy of the library media center staff are key factors for program success. The larger the library media center staff, the more central activities can be conducted. No matter how small the library media center staff is, some part of the central program should be in evidence.

SCHOOL-WIDE THEMES

Seasonal

A seasonal emphasis is an easy but effective way to begin flexible access resource-based teaching activities. All students can participate in activities, or "Holiday Happenings," through large-group, primary and intermediate storytimes and small-group, grade-appropriate centers. Figure 5.2 shows a sample holiday activities invitation. The winter center for first-grade students might have them alphabetize names by the first letter as they arrange stockings. Third-grade students might alphabetize the same stockings to the third letter or alphabetize the contents of the stocking. Second-grade students might tag the contents of holiday presents as part of a dictionary activity and fifth-graders might use the encyclopedia and an atlas to locate the country of origin of appropriate symbols.

Special Occasions

The library media staff can use special occasions or develop special celebrations in which all students and teachers can participate. During the months of December and January we run a membership drive for Caldecott Club, Newbery Club, and Sunshine Club. All students, parents, and staff are encouraged to participate. Those who complete the requirements for membership meet monthly for a variety of activities. The first meeting is a reception for all members. The next two meetings find members enjoying cooking and crafting items related to Caldecott, Newbery, or Sunshine State Young Readers' Award titles. The final meeting for the Caldecott and Newbery clubs is a reading picnic at which the most recent recipient of these awards is shared. The final Sunshine Club meeting, a Sunshine Luncheon, features only foods mentioned in the twenty titles on the year's list.

Special Events

Cultural arts programs planned by the parent-teacher organization can be introduced and reinforced through the library media program. Prior to showing students a marionette show, introduce all students by individual classes to puppetry and several versions of the fairy tale that is to be presented. After watching the program, students participate in grade-appropriate follow-up activities. These timely activities make your flexible access library media program visible to students, staff, and parents.

Fig. 5.2. Holiday Activities Invitation.

To: All Teachers

From: Jan Buchanan

Date: October 23, 1989

Re: Halloween Happening

You and your students are invited to a Halloween Happening in the Media Center on Tuesday, October 31. We will be reading and telling ghost stories, poems and riddles.

During your scheduled time we will be doing activities appropriate for your grade. You may schedule your entire class for the storytime or as a reward for selected students. The schedule is as follows: 11:00-12:00, 4 & 5 grades; 12:30-1:30, 2 & 3; and 2:00-3:00, PreK, K, and 1.

We will be giving the children a treat at the conclusion of the program and if you participate we ask that you please provide one ghost lollipop* per child. We suggest that you contact your teacher's helper for assistance in purchasing the necessary items and assembling the ghosts. We will need them by the afternoon of Monday, October 30.

Please let us know if you wish to be included.

*Directions for ghost lollipop:

> 1 Tootsie Roll pop or Dum Dum per child
> 1 facial tissue per child
> thin string
> fine tip black pen

Cover each lollipop with a tissue. Secure tissue with string to form ghost. Add eyes with marker.

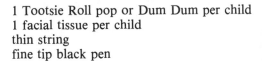

Many schools have a curriculum fair of student displays of topics studied by classes and individuals. The library media center can be the major supplier of materials and ideas and a place for displaying lessons. Other schools have fairs which focus on a school-wide theme such as medieval times or space technology. Here again, the library media center can both lead or support such themes with materials and activities leading up to the culminating event.

School Priorities

School-wide activities that reinforce a priority area of the curriculum are good starting points. If test scores indicate a weakness in science, the media program could emphasize experiences reinforcing that area of the curriculum. Often the principal already will have isolated a school-wide curriculum goal that can be targeted by the library media center. If not, you may wish to survey the faculty to determine those areas in which to concentrate your efforts. The survey should ask teachers to respond to three instructions:

1. List a unit or units you presently teach that you would like to expand.

2. List a unit or units that you would like to teach if you had some assistance with planning, materials, or ideas.

3. List a unit or units you would like to teach but never find time to include.

By collecting data from a simple survey such as this, a multidisciplinary team in our school determined that map and globe skills were high on the list of priorities of many primary and intermediate teachers. The resulting planning sessions generated activities to reinforce these skills through all areas of the curriculum. In addition to the activities they take part in in the classroom and the media center, our students participate in map and globe skills experiences in art, music, and physical education.

GRADE LEVEL THEMES

Initially you may want to plan a resource-based teaching unit for each grade that will be successful with each class in that grade. Ask each grade to select a topic for your first experiences. In many districts where basal readers are used, all students in a particular grade are exposed to each story in the text at some point in the year. Reading topics therefore are good choices for initial activities because they will be relevant to all students. For some students, the unit may be an introduction to the basal topic, while to others it may be a culminating activity. Others will probably respond, "That's what we read today!"*

---

*Figure 5.3 shows a sample of this type of unit. The central circle shows the story from the basal reader read in the classroom. The library media specialist and the teacher then extend that story in the library media center. Each box shows a supplementary book title which is used to teach a library or information skill. Select two or three additional topics on which to concentrate throughout the year.

Fig. 5.3. Resource-Based Teaching Unit 4: "Making Dreams Come True" (from Houghton Mifflin *Literary Readers, Book 4, Selection Plans and Instructional Support*, 1989).

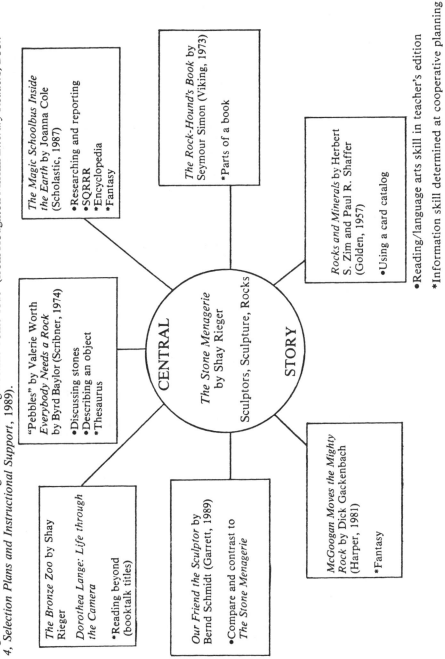

Our bedtime and sleep-out units were created with first-grade teachers to correlate with a unit in the basal reader used in our district. The first unit was planned to culminate with a pajama party in the media center, emphasizing the poetry and stories in the basal literature supplement. When I moved to another school in our district, the teachers also wanted to do the bedtime unit. Our library media center could not accommodate all the students for a pajama party and I did not want to duplicate an activity that had received so much attention at my former school. We did have a large, wooded area outside, which was perfect for our sleep-out. The story in the basal reader entitled "Sleep Out" was the inspiration to use another title of the same name, Carol Carrick and Donald Carrick's *Sleep Out* (Clarion, 1973). The Carrick title became the focus for our outdoor centers. The weekly centers remained essentially the same, while the storytimes reflected the sleep-out theme rather than the bedtime theme.

Determine what kinds of activities have the greatest appeal for teachers and students, then incorporate them into the unit plan. Plan center activities that occur for each class in first grade, for example, over a six-week period to allow time to begin preparation of activities for the topics selected for the other grades. Decide the schedule and responsibilities for the teacher and library media specialist during the cooperative planning session. Use the prepared materials for six weeks. Other than the time needed for evaluation and actual instruction time, you will be able to concentrate on activities for another grade. An example of such a schedule follows:

30 minutes	Week 1	Introduce unit to the class.
		Share large-group story.
		Demonstrate each of the four centers.
45 minutes	Week 2	Divide the children into media activity groups.
		Each group completes one center.
		Share large-group story lesson.
45 minutes	Week 3	Each group completes a second center.
		Share large-group story lesson.
45 minutes	Week 4	Each group completes a third center.
		Large-group storytime lesson.
45 minutes	Week 5	Each group completes the rotation and finishes all centers.
		Large-group storytime lesson.
2 hours	Week 6	Introduce culminating activities to the entire grade.
		Each child completes all centers.

INDIVIDUAL UNITS

Individual units of instruction are the heart of the library media center program. They are jointly planned by the teacher and the library media specialist. Ideas might come from the simple survey mentioned previously, from teacher planning sheets (see figure 4.3), from teacher conferences.

Using Commercial Sources

Each year hundreds of ideas for planning individual units of instruction are published by individual teachers, school districts, and commercial publishers. Teacher Ideas Press, a division of Libraries Unlimited, is one of many publishers whose materials link classroom topics and the library media center. A few of these titles are included in the "Additional Readings" section at the end of this chapter and in appendix E. For other suggestions of books with information skills application that can be incorporated into thematic units, see appendix F.

Library media specialists are wise to gather these types of idea sources for the professional library. Many of these ideas can form the basis of box units (see p. 45). An idea fair for teachers, focusing on ideas in commercial sources, might stimulate action and take some of the burden off the teacher and the library media specialist to create these units from scratch.

A Sample Resource-based Teaching Unit: Picture Dictionaries, First Grade

This is a teacher-initiated unit for first-grade students for an individual teacher's class. Before developing this unit, the teacher had participated in cooperative planning sessions with her grade level once a month. Her students' cooperatively planned library media experiences had been scheduled as large-group activities. The class was then divided into small groups for center work. To complete each of the centers, the class was scheduled for thirty minutes for three to five weeks. Shortly after one of our planning sessions the teacher entered the library media center, commenting, "I have a group of students who are finished with their reading books and I would like them to do an activity in the library media center." I remarked that these students had not yet had an opportunity for hands-on experience with the picture dictionaries and that they could create their own to share in the classroom. We decided that theirs would be a picture dictionary of transportation. This would be a perfect extension for their transportation unit. They had time to complete the project before their unit culminating activity, a train ride.

The group was scheduled for one hour each day for five days. There was little preparation for the unit. I placed pieces of paper with each letter of the alphabet in a bag so that the students could draw for the letters they would be researching and illustrating. The title page and dedication page were assigned as needed to give the students equal responsibility. On the first day we introduced the students to the arrangement of the picture dictionaries in our collection. The students located other books that would be helpful in compiling their own group book.

After a few minutes of modeling the students were ready to begin. They advanced rapidly from the picture dictionary to the unabridged dictionary as we searched for a mode of transportation beginning with such letters as **U** (*umiak*—an Eskimo boat) or **X** (*xebec*—a Mediterranean sailing ship). At this point the children and I discussed the amount of information they had been able to find. For several letters there were numerous modes of transportation, but for many it was difficult to find even one. They decided that their picture dictionary should change format and become an ABC book. (No, they did not find a type of transportation pictured for **Z**. Their book concludes with: "We've shown you things that can zip you from one place to another." The latest dictionary does picture a zeppelin.)

On successive days the children spent a minimum of an hour researching their letters, selecting the mode of transportation they wished to use, cutting their letters with the Ellison letter machine, and illustrating. The children were so engrossed in what they were doing during the first two days that the teacher and I agreed we should work with them longer. By Friday each child had completed the final draft of his or her contributions to the book. The students collated their *Transportation ABC*, bound it using the binding machine, and returned to class with a book their entire class enjoyed for the rest of the year.

A few weeks later the same teacher approached me and said, "Jan, I have a group that's almost finished with their reading book. Could you do picture dictionaries with them like we did with the other group?" The transportation unit was over, but the first graders were currently studying animals in science. We agreed that this group would prepare a picture dictionary of animals. The same procedure was followed, and near the end of the week each page of the book was filled with numerous animals, except for the letter **X**. For **X** we searched our science encyclopedias; from the few family names the student selected *xancidae*—a mollusk. Perhaps it is a word that was soon forgotten, but the search process was retained.

I was not surprised to see the teacher again in a few days, this time saying, "I have a group that will never finish their reading books but I want them to have this experience. They are the ones who don't complete their work and don't often get to do anything special." Much of the first-grade science curriculum dealt with living and nonliving things. These students created a picture dictionary of things (nonliving). Many spontaneous science lessons resulted from their questions during research: "Mrs. Buchanan, is an apple in the store a nonliving thing or is it living because the tree is a living thing?"

While the various groups of students were working on this project I had one of the experiences that reminds me why I choose to have a program that requires more time and effort than any rigid access program. As I stepped back from assisting a child and looked around the library media center I realized that each of the fifty or so children in the center at that time had been sent by their teacher for a specific purpose, not because it was the time that the principal had scheduled for them to "have library." I had not solicited any of the activity, the teachers had initiated it all. At lunch I described the experience to my principal and he laughingly responded, "Am I supposed to be impressed?" "Yes, you are," I answered. "You are supposed to be very impressed. It's what you and I say can happen, but today it was a reality. Today our teachers showed me a flexible access program."

A Sample Unit: Solar System, Fifth Grade

During our weekly cooperative planning session, one of the fifth-grade teachers mentioned that she would like each student to produce either a planet chalk drawing or a constellation picture, as students had done in the past. How did the library media program fit into this project? The students would first be researching their solar system topics. Since they had already had numerous experiences and were quite comfortable with the search process, we thought that only a few minutes' demonstration of specialized reference sources was necessary. They also would need an introduction to the opaque and overhead projectors, all of which could be accomplished in a thirty-minute full-class session. I thought that the solar system unit would be an excellent opportunity to introduce mythology to the students. Why didn't we have the students locate a myth connected with their planet or constellation and share it with the class? Introducing the characteristics of myths and the process for retrieving myths was included in the introductory lesson, which had now been extended to an hour.

The class was scheduled for an hour's large-group instruction, which was cooperatively taught by the teachers and myself. The students would be sent in small groups as convenient. It was not necessary that I know when, however, the teacher realized that a problem might occur if all small groups worked at the same time with our limited resources. The teacher arranged a schedule for small groups which could change daily if necessary. As the first students were ready to begin using the opaque or overhead projector, they were scheduled as individuals. After a small core of students was trained, the other students, accompanied by a trained student, used the equipment at the teacher's convenience. The planet drawings were chalked in the media production room under the supervision of fifth graders' volunteer parents. The constellation pictures (gummed stars on a black background or punch pictures on black) were completed in the media center reading room. The entire project took a month to complete, with frequent unscheduled assistance by the library media staff.

Hints for Resource-based Teaching

As the number of resource-based teaching units increases, scheduling problems might arise. Following are a few tips from our experience for pacing these units:

1. Schedule preparation for each unit in addition to instructional time. You will need the time to organize and orchestrate the units.

2. Schedule so that no two new centers or activities are introduced during the same week.

3. Be sure that both teachers and the library media staff are cooperatively teaching, executing, and evaluating the units. You are not there to teach units of instruction so that teachers can take a break.

4. Remember that instruction is only one responsibility of a library media specialist. Schedule responsibilities other than instruction so that your plan book or calendar reflects the total program. Enter time to do materials cataloging as you do instruction so that teachers will not feel you have "free time" and could schedule a class. For example, an hour block in your plan book might say:

   9:00-10:00 DDC

   Materials:

   Classification book

   Subject heading list

   Call labels

   Catalog cards

5. Schedule time for an introduction for the entire class or all students who will be doing the same small-group activities. While this can be done by the library media staff alone, it is much more effective when teachers participate in a team mode.

6. Videotape instructions for students when possible (for example, media center orientation, equipment demonstrations, directions for learning centers).

7. Audiotape lengthy center directions for primary students. Include appropriate pauses so that they can complete each step before proceeding to the next.

8. Be sure to evaluate the success of the unit with teachers. A little honesty about the time and effort that went into the unit in relation to the learning obtained from it will help both parties decide if the unit should be resource-based in the future.

CONCLUSION

The dynamic nature of the flexible access program constantly demands new responses to new situations. Regularly scheduled cooperative planning sessions enable the staff to address the issues, confront scheduling problems, and stay informed as students and staff explore alternatives. The program will never be static, yet you can reach a point in the development when you can say with confidence that the library media program has arrived. That point will be when there is a healthy mix of both ongoing and central program elements occurring simultaneously. When the library media center is packed to overflowing during most hours of the day, you know you have arrived.

PROFESSIONAL ACTIVITIES

1. Plan a school-wide activity to begin flexible access implementation in your school.

2. Plan a grade level activity for each grade to introduce flexible access to each grade in your school.

3. Plan several resource-based units of instruction, one using commercial sources and one with teacher-created materials.

4. Complete a calendar for one week, listing the central program activities and ongoing activities that require supervision by the library media staff.

ADDITIONAL READINGS

Barchers, Suzanne I. *Creating and Managing the Literate Classroom.* Englewood, Colo.: Libraries Unlimited, 1990.
Barchers shows teachers how to make the transition from traditional curricula to whole language or literature-based programs and how to include the library media center in those plans.

Butzow, Carol Ann, and John Butzow. *Science through Children's Literature: An Integrated Approach.* Englewood, Colo.: Libraries Unlimited, 1989.
Popular picture books with a science theme are used to build units that combine literature, science, language arts, art, etc. These units can be done in the library media center, the classroom, and in areas used by special teachers.

Doll, Carol A. *Nonfiction Books for Children: Activities for Thinking, Learning, and Doing.* Englewood, Colo.: Libraries Unlimited, 1990.
Suggests imaginative ways to integrate 55 high-quality nonfiction books for children into the curriculum, enriching the classroom and library media experiences.

McElmeel, Sharron L. *An Author a Month (for Pennies).* Englewood, Colo.: Libraries Unlimited, 1988.
Library media centers and classrooms can celebrate an author for an entire month without bringing that author to the school. McElmeel spotlights a number of authors using their books, writings, and illustrations as the basis for many classroom and library media center activities.

Toor, Ruth, and Hilda K. Weisburg. *Reasons, Roles, and Realities: A Hands-on Seminar in Resource Based Instruction*. Berkeley Heights, N.J.: Library Learning Resources, 1989.
    Toor and Weisburg not only provide a method of creating resource-based instruction, but also illustrate that method by providing numerous full-length units that can be used as is or modified.

Chapter 6

Winning Parents to a Flexible Access Library Media Program

This chapter will provide information to assist the library media specialist in:

1. *determining the level of parent involvement in a flexible access library media program and*

2. *developing a plan to achieve the desired level of involvement.*

The first step in winning parents to the flexible access library media program is determining what is wanted. Do you want parents merely informed, supportive, or involved? Decide which level of involvement you want, then develop a plan to attain it. Parents may either support the program or be actively involved in the library media program. Working with parents at each level requires time, effort and special communication by the media specialist. Parents will have a difficult time supporting something they know nothing about. You may wish to have periodic individual contact, group meetings to offer information, or the highest level of involvement: parent volunteers helping with certain tasks. You can obtain support without achieving involvement, but to acquire either, the media specialist must provide frequent information about what is being done in the media program and why. In some cases parent participation frees the library media specialist for other responsibilities. In other instances it provides parents with modeling experiences to share with their children. In all cases, parent participation can be the strongest public relations tool.

Winning parents is not very difficult if you address their concerns in ways they can understand. First, parents want to understand the program in relation to their children. Their next concern is "How can we help our children?"

What do their children do in the media center? Just saying that you have a "flexible access library media program" is certainly not sufficient to explain to parents what their children are doing. They need to know what the term means and why the school has adopted such a program. You can illustrate this most vividly with a video or slide presentation in which you inform parents of the hours of operation, cooperative planning, the types of activities they might expect in each grade, and how each of the aforementioned relate to the goal of the program.

We have used the script in figure 6.1 with slides to introduce a school's flexible access program to all parents at a parent-teacher association meeting.

Fig. 6.1. The Flexible Access Program: A Slideshow Script.

While being introduced, I imagined what each of you visualized as you probably remembered a library experience — intimidated by a stern-faced librarian with gray hair, bun, and spectacles speaking in whispers in the inner sanctum of a library.

Your children, I hope, will have very different memories. Some of the characteristics of the stereotype will still apply to some of us — the gray hair and the reading glasses. That is where the similarity will end, for we are developing independent library media users of our students — students who can articulate their desires and retrieve information vital to survival in their constantly changing environment. If you have had the opportunity to visit us you will know that this is happening in a far from hushed inner sanctum of a library but in a lively, bustling flexible access library media center.

Your child is welcome to explore the library media center every day before or after school and at the discretion of the classroom teacher during school hours.

In addition, each language arts class has a regularly scheduled time for checking books in and out.

We have a collection of over seventy-five hundred books and four thousand audiovisual materials which are carefully selected to insure quality materials for our students.

Each and every scheduled instructional lesson which your child has with the library media specialist has been planned with the teacher to insure the development of independent library media users.

Following a scope and sequence for information skills, lessons are planned cooperatively to correlate with all areas of the curriculum while emphasizing literature.

Some weeks your child may have a library media experience each day or several times in one day — in music, language arts, and social studies. Some weeks your child will have no scheduled library media instruction.

While planning with the teacher it is also decided if the objectives of the lesson can be most effectively met by large-group, small-group, or individual instruction.

In kindergarten, you can expect large-group storytime and small-group centers.

In first grade, there are center activities reinforcing skills with subject themes such as friendship, frogs, bedtime, and mice.

Each center in the library media center has an original theme-based game created to reinforce specific skills.

There are lots of listening and viewing activities and production activities — bookmarks, puppets, etc.

Many hours are spent by volunteers in preparing the thirty centers used with kindergarten, first, and second grades.

In second grade we continue to reinforce library media skills with centers emphasizing the elements of a story — character, plot, and setting.

Students begin a learning activity packet which introduces them to fiction and nonfiction, card catalog, and subject encyclopedias.

Koala Coupons provide practical application of all third-grade library media skills.

Students are introduced to the skills and coupons in large groups.

They complete each coupon independently and have their work checked by either the library media specialist, media assistant or, on occasion, the principal.

Fourth and fifth grades have large-group instruction encompassing literary genre and reference tools. After large-group instruction the students often decide to read a book from that particular genre and complete activities at centers.

Whether tall tales, fantasy, realistic fiction, fairy tales, or historical fiction, the student is able to complete activities using all modalities—listening, viewing, and doing.

After each reference tool is introduced, students locate information using those tools. The results of their research are limitless—a written report, a media production, or an oral presentation.

In addition to scheduled instructional time we stimulate students to be library media users with a variety of school-wide or grade-level activities and events.

Cooking, crafting, and reading are enjoyed by our three hundred Caldecott, Newbery, and Sunshine Club members.

Passports have encouraged students to read about other cultures through folktales, fiction, and nonfiction.

During Children's Book Week you may have noticed unusually dressed characters—that's the media staff making books come alive.

Students answer questions daily from the seasonal reference tree and enjoy activities in the Artist Nook and Composer Corner which highlight a different famous artist and composer each month.

Our CTBS scores reinforce that our flexible access library media program, which encourages practical application of skills, is working. Our students last year scored an average of 4.2 to 5 years above grade level, but more important are the observations I can make each day of the year of children who are developing a lifelong habit of reading and a love of learning—students who are prepared to meet the challenges of tomorrow because of each of our efforts today.

Last, but not least, the library media center serves as a learning laboratory for classroom instruction.

Teachers plan with the library media staff to use the resources of the library media center to teach science, social studies, language arts, math, and every other subject taught in the school.

These team-taught units of instruction go beyond what could be done in the classroom alone.

Subject specialists such as art, music, and P.E. teachers might contribute to a topical study based in the library media center.

This approach is called integrated learning—a chance to save precious time by correlating many topics into a single unit of instruction.

Please visit the library media center. And when you do, watch for individual and small groups of students streaming in and out of the library media center all day long.

Watch for small groups being instructed by the library media staff.

Watch for teachers working with groups of students on library media projects.

And, watch for the library media staff, teachers, and other subject specialists teaching a theme cooperatively.

We think you will like what you see! And if you do, why not volunteer to spend a few hours a week helping out?

The pay isn't great, but your contribution can be very rewarding.

Conclude the presentation by dividing into grade level groups and giving parents an opportunity to review the materials their children use or the products they make. If the presentation is part of a back-to-school night, have student assistants conduct tours of the library media center for parents.

The means for educating parents about the flexible access library media program in your school are the same as those employed for educating the staff. Unlike educating teachers, who must be in attendance at faculty workshops, not all parents will be at parent meetings. Spread the news through brochures, newsletters, and displays.

PARENT INVOLVEMENT IN DEVELOPING CHILDREN'S SKILLS

Once parents are informed about what their children are doing they often will be eager to know how they can support the program. They are less likely to participate (or participate with little enthusiasm) if the information or help which is requested is too general in nature. The media specialist must personalize all information disseminated to the parents and indicate specific ways parents can help. A presentation entitled "An Introduction to Elementary Media Skills" is not too inspiring. Interest can be expected if the information imparted is specific — "What Parents Need to Know about the Media Center" — and if the presentation is made in conjunction with other events which parents will be attending. School provides the child with the necessary skills for reading, but home is where the child can develop an interest in books and a love of reading. Parents are the first and foremost teachers, the primary role models. Parents must show that reading is important by making books and reading a part of the home.

Research indicates what many parents have known or at least suspected all along: children whose parents read to them become better readers. Many parents are aware that they should read aloud to their children, but they may not know how to find time to read or what to read. Establishing a nightly reading ritual makes reading to, with, and alongside family members a routine that produces numerous rewards. Many families have found that reading aloud to each other or reading together during the half hour before the children's bedtime is ideal. When children are old enough to read independently, this time can be used for all family members to read individually. These parents also encourage reading as a free time activity and allow children to choose their own reading materials. Criteria for selecting reading materials for children and techniques for reading aloud to children can be presented to parents in workshops or through printed materials.

Planning school-wide reading stimulation programs that involve parents either in reading with or to their child or just initialing a sheet to verify the titles read is a first step in encouraging parental involvement in reading. The American Association of School Librarians encourages every school to conduct an annual "Night of a Thousand Stars" activity to provide an evening of reading with local community dignitaries and parents.

Parents should be encouraged to set aside a time to visit the public library with their children. Insert public library information along with public library card applications in new student packets to show that the school places a high priority on reading.

Suggest that parents give books and magazines to their children as presents. A welcome gift to parents might be an annotated bibliography of appropriate materials, such as subject bibliographies (e.g., "If Your Child Loves Dinosaurs These Books Are Sure to Please," "For Budding Athletes," or "Just for Second Graders"). Display appropriate bibliographies and materials at parent meetings.

Promote the establishment of home libraries for families. Make recommendations to parents of books and ways to organize them and stress the importance of designating a special place for books. Children who have available a wide variety of reading materials—from books to magazines and newspapers—and a specific place set aside for them to read tend to take a greater interest in reading. Perhaps local bookstores might help with a particular activity by giving discounts as prizes or encouraging visits.

Some efforts have been made to assess students' views on parent participation in their reading activities. Anthony Fredericks, a reading specialist for the Catasauqua Area School District in Pennsylvania, conducted an informal survey of 93 third and fourth graders reading above grade level. The students were asked to list the things their parents did that they felt contributed to their reading success. In order of preference, their responses were as follows:

- Starting with easy books.

- Buying me lots of books.

- Turning off the television.

- Getting me a library card.

- Getting harder books for me later.

- Letting me read to them.

- Reading often to me.

- Sharing lots of children's books.

Although in the majority of families today both parents work and have few hours for active participation in the library media program, there are opportunities for active parent involvement. School community involvement leads to a sense of ownership of the program; shared ownership is vital to the success of a flexible access library media program.

You may wish to survey parents at the beginning of the school year so that you and they will be able to anticipate how they might help throughout the year. Then send notices to the appropriate parents asking for volunteers for specific projects and events. Structure activities so that parents know what to expect. When activities are planned for an entire grade level, such as a Teddy Bear's Picnic, ask parents to direct the centers to free teachers to supervise. Many parents who are unable to volunteer in the classroom or library media center on a regular basis are able to share one afternoon. Parents are often able to arrange to take a longer lunch hour to participate in a grade's read-a-thon as part of a school-wide activity. Invite parents to share one of their child's favorite stories or books with the class. Parents may assemble the costumes or treats for Holiday Happenings at home, then share the storytime with their child. As you would do with teachers, begin the year with an interesting parent/child event that will encourage continued participation.

Book fairs and book swaps provide opportunities for parents to work at school, actually manning the fair, or at home, tallying or organizing orders. Parents may prepare bulletin boards or displays for the library media center or other areas of the school. A parent may wish to assume responsibility for preparing a perpetual center that features a different Book of the Week, highlights new acquisitions, or focuses on selected authors. Parents often prepare center activities at home. All parents should be encouraged to participate in materials selection. Many additions have been made to our collection as a result of a parent sharing a title discovered at the public library or a bookstore.

SERVICES TO PARENTS

Just as the library media program thrives with parent support and involvement, so can the parents be served by a flexible access program. Resources are often made available to parents in a special parent section of the library media center. This collection might include tips on how and what to read, information on community cultural programs for children, and parenting materials. Provide parent orientation to the library media center so that parents are able to assist in selecting appropriate books for and with the children. Also provide a regular time or schedule specific times to be available for consultation with parents. When developing assignments and projects that require work outside of school, the library media specialist and the classroom teacher can alleviate much anxiety by providing a supplementary parent fact sheet.

MAINTAINING PARENT INTEREST

Instead of making a parent information campaign a one-time effort, conduct a continuous campaign. If your campaign spotlights not only what you do well but also what teachers do to utilize the resources of the library media center, emphasizing student progress, parents are much more likely to support the heavy investment a library media center program requires. The following hints might generate some ideas for the campaign:

1. *Keep parents well informed.* This may be done through newsletters, requests for help, or meetings.

2. *Communicate with parents regularly on a more personal basis.* Include information in grade level newsletters. Parent members of the library media advisory committee may disseminate appropriate information to the parents at each grade level.

3. *Create a consistent plan.* Be available at specific times for conferences. Schedule times that parents may visit the library media center. Plan parent activities on a regular basis. Publish newsletters at regular intervals.

4. *Design each meeting.* In each meeting, provide time to get and give information, encourage active participation, and show parents how to help their children.

5. *Realize that parent involvement may pertain only to an individual child.*

PROFESSIONAL ACTIVITIES

1. Plan a general education program to be used to introduce all parents to your flexible access library media program.

2. Develop a parent involvement plan for each grade level. The plan should include how the parents will be informed and what they will do.

ADDITIONAL READINGS

American Library Association. *Let's Read Together: Books for Family Enjoyment.* Chicago: American Library Association, 1985.

Binkley, Marilyn R. *Becoming a Nation of Readers: What Parents Can Do.* Washington, D.C.: U.S. Department of Education, 1988.

Copperman, Paul. *Taking Books to Heart: How to Develop a Love of Reading in Your Child.* New York: Addison Wesley, 1986.

Esworthy, Helen. "Parents Attend Reading Clinic, Too." *Reading Teacher* 32 (April 1979): 831-33.
Workshop suggestions for involving parents in children's reading development.

"Getting Parents Involved in Books for Children." *Reading Teacher* 32 (April 1979): 822-25.
Explains seven proposals developed by the Children's Book Council for involving parents in children's reading.

"If We Really Want Parent Involvement." *The Master Teacher* 17 (17 March 1986).

Kimmel, Margaret Mary, and Elizabeth Segel. *For Reading Out Loud: A Guide to Sharing Books with Children*. New York: Delacorte, 1988.

Larrick, Nancy. *A Parent's Guide to Children's Reading*. New York: Bantam, 1982.

Lipson, Eden Ross. *The New York Times Parent's Guide to the Best Books for Children*. New York: Times Books, 1988.

"News for Parents." *Reading Today*. Newark, Del.: International Reading Association.
　　This single-page newsletter for parents appears six times a year as part of the International Reading Association membership publication, *Reading Today*. Dissemination of the information to parents is encouraged and any or all of the page may be reprinted without permission.

Reading Is Fundamental. Department 106. 600 Maryland Avenue SW, Washington, D.C.
　　RIF publishes a series of brochures to encourage reading at home. "Summertime Reading," "Building a Family Library," and "Family Storytelling" are available for bulk purchase and would be excellent for distribution at an open house.

Russell, William F. *Classics to Read Aloud to Your Children*. New York: Crown, 1984.

Trelease, Jim. *The Read-Aloud Handbook*. New York: Penguin, 1985.

Wilson, Mary E. "Reading: A Family Affair." *School Library Journal* 35 (November 1989): 48.
　　A successful celebration of Childrens Book Week in which parents were invited to a "Reading Is a Family Affair" where they participated in miniworkshop sessions and watched students perform.

Chapter 7

Evaluating Flexible Access Library Media Programs

This chapter provides information to assist the library media specialist in:

1. *identifying quantitative and qualitative measurements for evaluating flexible access library media programs and*

2. *selecting appropriate summative evaluation tools.*

When radical changes are made in any organization, there is usually strong pressure to determine whether or not the changes measure up to the forecasts made for them. In social organizations, which do not have cars coming off an assembly line or a profit and loss statement at the end of each month, evaluation is somewhat more difficult, but just as necessary, as it is in business.

Two types of evaluation measures are discussed in the sections that follow: *summative* and *formative*. Summative evaluations are done at the conclusion of an activity or program. For example, teachers might be given a questionnaire on how well the resource-based teaching unit succeeded. The questionnaire is distributed at the conclusion of the unit. At that point, it is too late to do anything to correct any problems, but the information gathered will be valuable in planning future units.

Formative evaluation measures are taken while an activity is in progress. For example, if you notice that the students are bored during a storytelling session, you could pick up the pace of the story, use more expression in your voice, or abandon that story and use another in its place. In chapter 3, a needs assessment was suggested as a prelude to beginning a flexible access program. This evaluation could be considered a formative one, since it measures the possible success of a proposed change that is not yet in effect.

In education, both library media specialists and teachers must be sensitive enough to student needs and feelings to adjust instructional plans immediately to the requirements of both groups and individuals. Those who are blinded by their own patterns of teaching take the risk of enacting the famous book title, *The Geranium on the Window Sill Just Died, But the Teacher Went Right On*. If children show a lack of interest when you read out loud, it is time to either

109

improve your read-aloud skills or do some other activity. The power of discernment is a gift to be cultivated throughout a career.

The library media specialist and the library media advisory committee together formulate the tools for measuring and the methods and procedures for conducting the assessment of program strengths and weaknesses. The assessment is then conducted involving users (teachers, students, parents, and administrators). The evaluation should be both quantitative and qualitative. The data gathered are analyzed and the program is modified based on the results. In addition to the obvious changes that are indicated, the results can assist in decision making; be used to revise goals, objectives, and policies; facilitate communication; be used to define roles; and be used to design user education programs.

QUANTITATIVE MEASUREMENTS

Attendance and Circulation

Both attendance and circulation can be expected to increase with a flexible access library media program. A simple sign-in system may be used to determine unscheduled small-group and individual use (see figure 7.1). In one school, the library media specialist and the teachers decided to use the form suggested here. They wanted to be sure the children were getting to the library once a week, to forestall any recommendation for scheduled class visits from an accreditation team that was coming in the next month. After a thirty-day use of the form by all children, the library media staff took score. Not only had every child in the school been in the library media center at least once a week, but some students had been in as often as five times a day!

One of the requirements in our information skills curriculum is that children come to the library media center with a purpose. This is constantly reinforced as they are asked to indicate on the sign-in sheet why they are using the library media center. The number of students attending scheduled large-group or class instruction or activities may be recorded in your plan book. If you use a computer for students to record their attendance, you certainly will not have students forgetting to sign-in.

If statistics are not maintained with an automated circulation system, you may wish to do periodic checks of those items returned rather than dedicate time on a daily basis to maintaining circulation records. When using manual checkout procedures, select three or four "normal" weeks during the school year to count those items returned to determine the approximate number of materials circulated during the year. The same thing can be done if your circulation system allows for counting the number of materials checked out during selected weeks. Time is better spent in a flexible access program on activities other than circulation statistics. However, you will want to know if circulation is greater under your flexible program than under a rigid one.

Fig. 7.1. Student Response Form.

Name	Become a Media Expert	Koala Coupon	Research	Media Skills Center	Check Out	Free Time	Other
Teacher's Name _____ Week _____
WHY ARE YOU HERE? By your name, please check the reason or reasons you are in the library media center today.

Participation

Student, staff, and community participation in voluntary activities is an effective means of evaluating the program. For example, the number of students participating in our recreational reading programs has shown a dramatic increase each year. These voluntary programs are designed for parents and children to discover the joy of shared reading. Teachers who accept the offer for their students to participate in our Holiday Happenings share in the reading of poems and stories. Our administrators have been known to change schedules to participate in these special programs. Parents have taken time from their work to enjoy library media activities with their children. In the evaluation of each individual activity, student, staff, and parent participation is recorded.

Lesson Plans, Schedules, and Administrative Duties

Lesson plans of both the teachers and the library media specialist can be used to evaluate instruction in a flexible access program. Evaluate both summatively (after the unit is complete) and formatively (during the unit). The content of the plans should indicate that:

1. Cooperative planning is scheduled and is occurring and that an array of activities results from this planning. Teacher lesson plans reflect the use of the library media program in teaching.

2. Information skills instruction is integrated into the curriculum and follows a scope and sequence. Appropriate skills are taught through each area of the curriculum using a variety of techniques and strategies.

3. A strong literature-based program is evident. Literature is used to teach information skills and opportunities are provided that encourage reading for pleasure.

You can use a tally sheet to record the frequency of instruction, technical duties, public relations activities, or cooperative planning sessions for a designated period of time. For example, the following data might be compiled:

*   *Skills instruction:*

    Amount of scheduled instructional time per teacher

    Amount of instructional time per grade

    Percentage of library media specialist's time spent in instruction for all students

    Amount of instructional time per skill

    Scope of skills presented

    Amount of time spent in preparation for instruction

- *Technical duties:*

  Amount or percentage of time spent selecting materials

  Amount of time spent cataloging materials

  Amount of time spent processing materials

- *Public relations:*

  Number of workshops or in-services presented

  Staff and parent population participating

- *Cooperative planning:*

  Frequency of teacher contact (informal)

  Number of scheduled sessions with teachers

  Actual amount of time spent planning with teachers

  Attendance and participation in curriculum meetings

  Number of teacher requests for materials or instructional assistance

The data collected from the flexible access program can then be compared to data from previous years under a rigid access program. You should see an increase in the frequency of skills instruction and cooperative planning activities.

Expenditures

An increase in the library media program budget, although desirable, is not necessary to have an effective flexible access program. However, allocation of additional monies to the program is an indicator of strong administrative support. Expenditures should reflect user input into the purchase of appropriate materials to enhance the school's flexible access program.

Standardized Tests

Norm-referenced tests may be the simplest method of judging the effectiveness of instruction, but they are not always the most accurate. Children taught in nontraditional library media centers may score slightly lower on commonly used standardized tests as a result of the test being geared to "old ways." For example, if the children are using an automated catalog but are still being tested on recognizing catalog cards, they may score lower. Likewise, some children may not have been taught guide words in a dictionary because this technique was not covered in a correlated approach. Children may have been quizzed on specific reference skills, such as collation on a catalog card or which reference book to use to answer a specific question, but not on the concept or application of the skills.

During the first year at my current school, we were thrilled at the independent library media use our students were exhibiting. A few weeks prior to the administration of a standardized test, it occurred to us that our students might have a different problem than the students for whom the TIC TOC (Totally Integrated Curriculum Through Open [Media] Center) program was originally created: They might not be able to respond correctly when asked to provide a single-word answer rather than show mastery of application of the skill. The impact of a flexible access program on standardized test scores is often negligible for the first few years. However, over several years, if the school population is relatively stable, the scores should show a marked increase when children are constantly interacting with library media materials as a part of their curriculum. Figure 7.2 compares reference skills scores in 1978 under a rigid access program to scores from 1982 and 1984 under a flexible access program. Students at all grade levels scored a minimum of two grade levels above the anticipated grade equivalent.

Fig. 7.2. CTBS Reference Skills Test Scores (1978, 1982, and 1984).

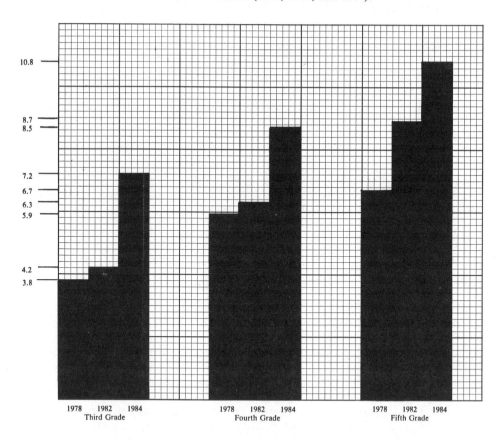

QUALITATIVE MEASUREMENTS

Written Evaluations

Written evaluations should include all users and participants in the library media program. Statistics can be compiled from written evaluations, but the written evaluations are most useful for assessing the quality of the services and activities provided. Each category should have an evaluation designed to assess those areas to which the group could most effectively respond.

Done by the Teacher. The teacher's evaluation (see figure 7.3) should not only cover the library media specialist's role but also ask questions to determine the teachers' understanding of their role in a flexible access library media program. If designed in this manner, the survey also is an educational tool that asks teachers to reflect on the behaviors they should exhibit. Regardless of the thoroughness of the survey, always solicit comments and suggestions. Teachers tend to include those things about which they feel most strongly and which they may not have had an opportunity to express elsewhere in the survey. React first to their comments and concerns, both positive and negative, to provide immediate feedback; this approach often assures that the appropriate program changes will be readily accepted. You can then analyze the results of the specific questions and make modifications as necessary.

During the development of our flexible access program the teacher evaluations were indispensable. Those evaluations are responsible for our having three options for student checkout today. I had envisioned in my "ideal" program that all children would use the library media center at the time of need and that there would be no checkout schedule; each student would circulate materials as appropriate. One teacher responded, "I would like to have a regularly scheduled time for student checkout each week. It seems my class was unable to utilize the come and go approach independently."

Another teacher remarked, "I would like to have a regularly scheduled time per teacher when there is no other class in the library media center for checkout at that time." Yet another commented, "I would like to send my students for checkout as a group so they can come one reading group at a time." Based on these comments, students may now have checkout as an entire class when no other class is scheduled for checkout and teachers may send students in small groups.

When the teachers at a grade level wrote, "sequential order is lost," I realized that the scope and sequence of information skills I had given the grade level chairman had not been disseminated. I now have as the first item on the agenda for the initial cooperative planning session for the year to distribute individual copies of the scope and sequence to each teacher and to explain how the skills checklist is used.

Done by the Student. The student evaluation (see figure 7.4) should indicate the extent to which the student has access to the library media center. Obviously those students who have not had the opportunity to use the library media center for a variety of purposes and in various-sized groups may not provide responses as valid as those of other students. Create a survey to assess primary students and another for intermediate students.

(Text continues on page 119.)

Fig. 7.3. Teacher Library Media Program Evaluation.

Date _____

Please indicate for each of the items below the response that most accurately reflects your feelings and experiences.

Y for yes   N for no   X for not applicable

1. Do you use the library media center for:

____ individuals sent from your classroom at any time?

____ small groups sent from your classroom at any time?

____ small groups sent from your classroom by appointment?

____ scheduled class visits for instruction?

____ scheduled class visits for circulation?

____ class use upon request?

____ your own use?

____ other? Please explain. _____

2. Does the library media specialist consult with you for instructional planning as:

____ an individual teacher?

____ part of a team, department, or grade level?

____ a member of a curriculum committee?

3. In planning for instruction with your library media specialist, do you:

____ have a regularly scheduled planning time?

____ make appointments for planning sessions as needed?

____ complete planning sheets, if requested, prior to planning?

____ assist in the selection and evaluation of materials?

____ involve the library media specialist in instructional activities using library media materials/technology?

____ have difficulty in scheduling the library media center for the lessons or units planned?

____ participate in the evaluation of library media center-based lessons or units?

____ inform the library media specialist of assignments that call for use of media resources?

4. As a result of cooperative planning with the library media specialist, do you notice:

____ more planning within and across grade levels?

____ increased sharing of materials by teachers?

____ increased teacher creativity?

____ information skills integrated with unit topics?

____ materials and technology used to better advantage?

5. In our school, our flexible access library media program:

____ follows an information skills scope and sequence.

____ provides relevant learning experiences for students.

____ provides opportunities for simultaneous activities in the library media center for more than one class.

____ encourages students to enter the library media center with a purpose.

____ encourages students to be independent library media users.

____ stimulates attendance in the library media center.

____ stimulates student circulation of materials.

____ stimulates staff circulation of materials.

____ is a positive experience for students.

____ is a positive experience for staff.

COMMENTS/SUGGESTIONS:

Fig. 7.4. Student Evaluation.

1. I am in grade _____.

2. I have been to our library media center:

    _____ by myself.

    _____ with a small group.

    _____ with my class.

    _____ with my grade.

3. I use our library media center:

    _____ when I need to.

    _____ when I want to.

    _____ only when the rest of my class does.

    _____ for pleasure reading.

    _____ for reports.

    _____ for centers.

4. I would use the library media center more often if:

    _____ I could find the materials and information I need.

    _____ the library media center had the materials I need.

    _____ the library media center had the materials I like.

    _____ the library media center were open longer hours.

    _____ I could come during class.

5. What I like best about our library media center is

    _____

    _____

    _____ .

6. What I like least about our library media center is

    _____

    _____

    _____ .

We have made many adaptations to practices, procedures, and even instruction as a result of student responses to the open-ended questions. I knew that I needed additional explanations for the card catalog when one of our younger students wrote that what he liked least about the library media center was: "Nobody takes the cards from the card catalog when they are checked out." With the advent of our electronic catalog I no longer have to remember to include this explanation in initial card catalog experiences. Some responses, such as "shelves are too high," did not effect change in library media center facilities, but we did purchase additional step stools and request that the district consider the height problem in the specifications for the next school. Other responses we could only smile at, such as "You can't go during weekends."

If you use specific rather than open-ended questions, you may wish to supervise completion of the evaluation. This provides the opportunity to explain any terms or skill designations with which the students are unfamiliar. One year, even though all intermediate students had been provided instruction in the operation of audiovisual equipment, I was surprised to learn from the evaluation that none of them had received such instruction! They did not sleep through instruction, they just did not realize that the overhead and opaque projectors were audiovisual equipment. The data would have been puzzling had I not administered the evaluation myself rather than have the classroom teacher do it.

Done by the Parent. The parent or community evaluation may focus on student behaviors, assess the flexible access program in the affective domain, or determine the effectiveness of library media communication and parent education programs. Are the parents aware of when their children have access to the library media center? Do the children use the library media center at various times each week for circulation and instruction? Do the children feel comfortable using the library media center? Why or why not? What is one library media center activity in which a parent's child participated that he or she enjoyed?

The parent representatives on the library media advisory committee are especially useful in creating the community assessment form. Not only will you be able to include items to evaluate established program priorities related to parents and the community, but you can also evaluate other relevant areas that have surfaced in parent meetings or through conversations with parents.

If the school already has a parent survey, you may wish to add relevant items to the existing questionnaire rather than create a separate form. The return of parent responses will probably be greater if library media data are gathered from a survey disseminated through the classroom teachers. Data may also be collected continuously through the year by including a feedback section with each school newsletter to solicit parent comments and reactions to upcoming and ongoing activities offered through the library media program. This tear-out portion of the newsletter allows for immediate response to needs and concerns rather than waiting until the start or finish of the year.

Done by the Principal. A written evaluation by the principal is necessary only if the instrument with which you are evaluated does not address the services and activities involved in a flexible access program. The tool used should be a simple checklist or one which requires minimal comments. The checklist may ask for a rating of "effective, adequate, or needs improvement" for areas such as activities, arrangement of facilities, teacher education, etc. Another form may state the goals and objectives or the priorities for the year and ask for strengths and weaknesses or the positives and negatives observed. Figure 7.5 is an example of a principal's assessment of a goal statement.

Fig. 7.5. Flexible Access Library Media Program: Principal Evaluation.

The goal of Wilson Elementary School's flexible access library media program is to develop independent media users.

What have you observed that has furthered this goal?

What have you observed that hinders the attaining of this goal?

_____

Done by the Library Media Advisory Committee. The library media advisory committee is charged with developing the evaluation instruments to be used in program evaluation and analyzing the data. Obviously, when discussing the instruments and the data you will receive informal evaluations from each member of the committee. You may wish to assess the members further by designing a written evaluation that focuses on the role of the committee and elicits comments and suggestions to enhance that role.

Done by the Library Media Staff. You may use the media program evaluation tool (figure 7.6) to evaluate the current status of the program. This quick checklist will assist in setting your personal goals each year. Dating it is a simple means to chart your progress in implementing and maintaining the program.

Observation

You may acquire additional qualitative data from observation of users, facilities, materials, activities, and projects. Record this information in a notebook, in lesson plans, or on the calendar.

Observe Users. Attendance records indicate the number of students and staff using the library media center, but only through observation can you determine the strategies that patrons use to locate, apply, and synthesize information. Users should feel comfortable when requesting assistance. Offer and provide individual assistance to learners as they use materials. Students should show excitement about what they are doing. The teaching staff should project a positive attitude toward media experiences and incorporate library media materials in their teaching. The transfer of learning from the elementary school library media center to the public library or middle school library media center is further evidence of the effectiveness of the program.

Observe Facilities. Attendance does increase with a flexible access program, and although observation can be used to determine the extent to which the library media center is used, it should be coupled with attendance records. Invariably during our first year of a flexible access program the library media center would be devoid of students when the principal walked through. In such instances I usually called the administrative office and asked him to come back. I often do attendance spot checks and record them in my plan book when it appears as if nothing is happening because no instruction or circulation is scheduled at that particular time.

The facilities should be arranged to accommodate both large and small groups. The traffic flow should allow for simultaneous browsing, listening and viewing, and instruction.

Flexible access library media programs further encourage use by providing attractive displays and appropriate directional signs. A student comment to me expressing the wish to "take a magazine" was the impetus for displaying a sign reminding students of checkout of magazines. The library media center should be orderly and well organized. Students and staff can help keep the library media center in order if all materials are organized with their participation in mind and have designated places.

Observe Materials in Use. Simultaneous use of the facilities implies that materials are also in constant use. You should see both materials being used in the library media center and a variety of materials being circulated. Materials should be of high quality and appropriate for the collection.

Observe the Activities. The flexible access program should provide active media experiences. Students are responsible for learning; independent activities are self-directing. Center activities should vary learning modalities.

Observe Student Success. Perhaps the most valid evaluation of all requires the least amount of time. This is the observation of student success rather than the statistics, the number of complaints, or the number of positive comments, the observation of students who are independent media users. When you see students who are proud of the quality and creativity of their work, who are confident in the library media center, and who continue to use the library media center to satisfy their information needs and for pleasure, you are seeing evidence of a successful program.

Fig. 7.6. Library Media Program Evaluation.

Date _____

Indicate for each of the items below the response that most accurately reflects the current status of your library media program.

	Effective	Adequate	Needs Improvement
Goals and objectives			
Policies and procedures reflect curriculum-integrated philosophy			
Knowledge of school's curriculum			
Familiarity with textbooks			
Familiarity with teaching styles of your teachers			
Written list of services			
Print and nonprint collection for resource-based units			
Circulation system			
Facilities arranged for flexible access			
Organization of teaching materials for easy access and curriculum integration			
Use of scope and sequence of information skills			
Tracking system for what skills are taught, to whom, and when			
Teacher preparation/introduction to the flexible access library media program			
Teacher/student handbooks			

Teacher/library media specialist planning schedule			
Use of cooperative planning sheet			
Cooperative planning sessions			
Information skills instruction related to classroom activities			
Simultaneous use of the media center for a variety of activities and by different age levels			
Individual use of the media center			
Small-group use of the media center			
Large-group/class use of the library media center			
Communication with administrators			
Methods of program evaluation			

COMMENTS AND SUGGESTIONS:

WHAT TO DO IF ...

Attendance Does Not Increase

Once the implementation of a flexible access library media program is inevitable, teachers often move from resisting the program because of what is perceived as loss of planning time and services to concern that the library media program now encroaches on valuable time needed to cover subject area content. How can the prescribed amount of subject matter possibly be covered in the prescribed amount of time if the students are always out of the classroom for special programs? To counter this reaction, provide each teacher with a copy of the information skills scope and sequence, with the skills that are included in the basal or subject area curriculum for that grade level highlighted. The highlighted scope and sequence graphically represents that the information skills curriculum is not separate from but very much a part of the classroom curriculum.

Offer to plan activities with teachers to reinforce, remediate, or expand those media-related skills for which they are responsible. Suggest various ways of grouping the students and means of completing media activities while the classroom teacher covers subject content. For example, after administering the periodic tests provided with the basal reading series, the teacher may become aware that several students are having difficulty in distinguishing "real and unreal." At this point you could provide remedial activities for those students. In another instance, you may introduce the section of the language text that deals with the card or online catalog while the teacher is responsible for testing the students and referring individual students for remediation.

At other times you may extend learning by providing literary genre centers so that students will have additional experiences in the library media center. Introduce historical fiction to the class with a selection in the text and make available for small groups extension activities based on other historical fiction titles.

A complaint often made by teachers and administrators about flexible access library media programs is that children need but do not have the routine and regularity of media experiences once afforded by the fixed schedule. Flexible access does allow for a routine of regular experiences, but it is a routine developed by the individual teacher based on the individual class. Cooperatively planned experiences are developed to meet the learning needs of the students as identified by the teacher. The teacher may choose to have you introduce the class to reference sources as a large group and then schedule small groups for research using the tools that were demonstrated.

Circulation Does Not Increase

If the schedule was not teacher-generated, the times assigned may not be the most convenient. Review the schedule to make sure that the teachers are indeed using the times for which they are scheduled. If not, offer to help them determine the best option for their students to regularly circulate books. Reiterate at various times throughout the year that the teacher can change a checkout option at any time

Many teachers think circulation should be entirely the library media specialist's responsibility. The library media specialist is responsible for small-group or individual checkouts. There are some teachers who will choose to have large-group checkout and they therefore choose to be responsible for their students' circulation. To make this job more palatable, offer suggestions to expedite checkout. Recognize those teachers who do an exemplary job and share their techniques with others.

Teachers may think that their students are short-changed if you do not assist with each checkout. To counter this impression, use literature-based programs to continuously reinforce selection skills with students. Pull related books for subject area study for each grade and place them on a cart. Change displays frequently to aid students in selection.

Participation Does Not Increase

Examine the educational programs employed for students, staff, and parents. Plan school-wide and/or grade level activities and invite all teachers, parents, and children to participate. Some teachers and parents think that only dull library media skills lessons occur in the library media center. Plan jointly with those teachers for "fun" experiences, maybe cooking once a month or having students create or contribute to displays on a regular basis.

Cooperative Planning Is Scheduled, But ...

1. *Teachers do not attend planning sessions*. In such cases you must be flexible. You should take the initiative by asking the teacher for a specific time to discuss a specific relevant activity. This may or may not be at the regularly scheduled planning time. Inquire if another time for planning is more suitable than the one the teacher originally selected, or offer to schedule various times.

   For the teacher who bemoans loss of planning time, make sure the benefits of cooperative planning are immediately evident. Capitalize on your roles as information specialist and instructional consultant. Provide a high level of information, ideas, and services so that teachers receive more than they are giving up in time.

2. *Teachers do not return planning sheets*. A reminder in the school newsletter or other communication usually solves this common problem. For those teachers who need an additional prod, an announcement by the principal over the public address system is quite effective.

3. *Teachers do not schedule activities*. It may be necessary initially to plan lessons independently and ask reluctant teachers to schedule a time for the predetermined activity. Often after the children have had such experiences in the library media center they will goad their teachers to schedule additional activities. The problem may be that the teacher is uncertain about what to schedule or how the schedule actually operates. The initial lessons may be those that you choose to model so the teacher can observe the program in action.

4. *Teachers do not plan original activities.* "I want to do what they're doing." is often heard during multiparticipant planning sessions. To combat this, have students repeat the purpose for which they are in the library media center at the beginning of each activity and/or ask the teacher to be responsible for students completing appropriate prerequisite skills prior to being scheduled.

5. *Teachers do not remember scheduled time.* It is best to decide prior to the time of need how and when teachers want to be reminded if they forget scheduled instruction time. You may suggest calling over the intercom or sending a note. Invariably after a note is written, the messenger passes the class in the hallway arriving a few minutes late. Waiting for ten minutes to be certain that the teacher has actually forgotten and is not just a few minutes late often poses a scheduling problem with the classes that follow. During the first year of our flexible access program I received a note at 11:20 from a teacher who was scheduled for a lesson from 11:00 to 11:30. It read "Forgot my media lesson. Could you do anything in fifteen minutes?" I responded that I could do several things in fifteen minutes, but none of them were the lesson we had planned. I asked for a convenient time to reschedule the lesson. For teachers who habitually forget or for all teachers during the first few months of flexible scheduling, you may wish to print a reminder that can be clipped into the teachers' plan books.

6. *Teachers do not remain with their classes.* Remind teachers of expected behaviors at a planning session. When the teacher returns to pick up the students, you might say "While you were gone...." Teachers are more willing not only to stay but also to participate if specific responsibilities have been determined during the planning session. When the teacher is not integral to the success of the activity, suggest a different activity for the teacher to do while you work with the students.

7. *The library media specialist is doing all the preparation for cooperatively planned experiences.* It is inherent in the program that the library media specialist bear the burden of the program during the initial stages. Take every opportunity to tactfully suggest those areas where the teachers planning the activities might assist; eventually they will offer to help. Ask teachers to help solicit parent participation or to allow students to help as appropriate.

Time for Technical Duties and Other Responsibilities Is Scarce

Be flexible, set priorities, don't expect perfection, and don't let little things become large problems. Decide what is important and what is not. There is a great deal you could worry about; choose only the major problems and those things you can control. Relinquish tasks that do not have to be done by you, such as preparing displays. Students enjoy working from a printout to pull materials for display. Not only will they help you, but they will be proud to show others "their" display. Schedule management tasks in your plan book as well as instruction time.

Test Scores Do Not Improve

Allow sufficient time for the program to affect scores and make sure that the populations being compared are similar. Use the terminology that will appear on the test during instruction.

Evaluations Are Negative

Administer the evaluation several times during the year rather than only once. Ask teachers to assist in setting priorities and solving the problems identified.

The Noise Level and Behavior in the Library Media Center Are Inappropriate

Although it is often uncomfortable to correct a class in the charge of another teacher, it may be as uncomfortable for the teacher to correct students in your territory, the library media center. Review the rules with all teachers, perhaps in a memo. Tell them you will be correcting any student in the library media center who is not following the rules and ask them to do the same. Select a means to alert students that the noise level is not acceptable. If after these measures a problem still exists, address it at a faculty meeting. Ask the teachers to help solve this problem that exists in "our" library media center.

The Library Media Center Is Left in Disarray

When this occurs after a class activity, appoint helpers from the class to make sure chairs are pushed in and shelves are straightened. Use "SOS" (Straighten Our Shelves) signs to indicate where additional help is needed.

Suppose you have done everything necessary to prepare yourself, the students, and the staff for your flexible access program, but it is still not working the way you envisioned. Problems will continue to arise and there will be some teachers who resist and reject certain aspects of the program. Success with your flexible access library media program is possible if you have a positive attitude and expect it to work. Don't give up, try a new approach. Don't take problems personally. Finally, keep your sense of humor.

PROFESSIONAL ACTIVITIES

1. Make a list of evaluation instruments to be used to assess the priorities you established for your program in chapter 3.

2. Develop the evaluation instruments listed for activity 1.

3. Obtain your school's standardized test scores for the past three years. Chart these scores as a basis for determining the impact of the flexible access program in your school. Plot each succeeding year's test scores.

Chapter 8

District-wide Flexible Access Library Media Programs

This chapter will provide information to assist the library media specialist in:

1. *determining ways district library media personnel can help with building level implementation of flexible access library media programs and*

2. *developing a district-wide implementation plan.*

Although phrased in different terms in each district across the country, each has as its goal "to develop lifelong learners." What better place to do that than in the library media centers throughout the district? When superintendents and other personnel at the district level in charge of library media programs are committed to offering the best library media center programs possible, they become key players in implementing the flexible access program in every school. Personnel with such a vision and such a support system are described by Carolyn Cain, a district library media director in the Madison, Wisconsin schools:

> The Madison Metropolitan School District has endorsed a broad program of library services for all its students. This philosophy is supported with sizable collections, adequate facilities and full time library media specialists in each building. The goal, as stated in the K-12 Program intent document, is as follows: "The library media program is an integral part of the overall instructional program of the school district. It provides resources and activities to meet the learning needs of all students. Its unified approach to all types of instructional media assures the greatest possible number of individual learning alternatives. Through joint planning between classroom teachers and library media specialists, its resources contribute to the effective design and implementation of a school's curriculum."

As school LMC's have striven to reach these program goals in recent years they have increasingly adopted a practice called flexible scheduling. For flexible scheduling to be successful, each school must be able to determine its own schedule for use of the LMC based on the instructional needs of the students. Situations in which principals are required to consider scheduled LMC classes as a way to provide guaranteed planning time for teachers are not consistent with this philosophy.[1]

How can a district acquire the vision evident in the district program outlined above? Such commitment does not come about overnight. The same hard work necessary to establish a flexible access program at the building level is needed at the district level. Should one begin at the district or at the school level to achieve change? There is probably no one way to proceed, for each school district in the United States is a political entity with pride in its autonomy. Thus, how one proceeds will be a political decision based on local needs, political climate, and local interests.

If you are able to begin at the district level, you can do a number of things at that level to instigate flexible access programs at the building level. Following is a list of some of these actions:

1. Share the various goals, objectives, and priorities of flexible access library media center programs that have been established in individual schools. If there are none, form a committee to develop suggested goals and objectives.

2. Compile a list of teacher and student library media center services offered in individual schools. Individual library media specialists can then use this complete list to survey their patrons and develop their own lists.

3. Solicit copies of evaluation instruments created by library media specialists in the district and around the country. Distribute a packet of these to library media specialists to use in developing their own tools.

4. Develop a library media policies and procedures framework, which each school can adapt to its particular situation.

5. Develop a sample scope and sequence of information skills. To do this, the district library media personnel may:

    a. Obtain funding for a curriculum writing team.

    b. Provide sample district and state level documents to aid in the development of the scope and sequence.

    c. Gain school board approval of the completed document.

6. Develop a flexible access program position statement or information paper. The state or regional library media association may assume this responsibility, or the district library media personnel may initiate the position statement. The district should gain board approval of the statement. Copies should be distributed to all district level personnel, the teachers' union, all principals, and all building level library media specialists.

7. Alleviate time-consuming technical responsibilities of building library media specialists. You can do this by providing centralized processing, automated systems, and any other support that allows the library media specialist to devote time and energy to the cooperative planning and implementation of relevant activities.

8. Work to fund library media center programs at exemplary levels. The district school board plays a crucial role in a flexible access program by providing sufficient funding for staffing. The staffing must provide contractual planning time for all teachers, separate from the library media center program, and adequate library media staff to allow a full range of services to be offered. The district level personnel also must procure funding for training, attendance at professional conferences, and release time for teachers and library media specialists.

9. Provide support groups. Encourage those schools with flexible access programs to meet periodically to discuss concerns and share ideas. The focus and participants attending could vary with each meeting. Involve administrators in problem solving areas of concern relevant to their positions and include the teachers' perspective when appropriate.

CREATING AN EFFECTIVE IN-SERVICE PROGRAM

When a number of schools attempt to change to flexible access programs, the district level library media staff can help immensely by instituting an effective in-service program. This program will be of use not only in effecting change but also in monitoring its progress and fine tuning the program in schools where problems arise. Developing an effective in-service program is the same at the district level as at the building level. The following points should serve as a checklist as the program is developed:

1. *Decide on the purpose of the in-service.* Is it to implement specific training or to allow the participants to set objectives for themselves and their respective schools?

2. *Who will do the training?* Will the district staff, a consultant, or building level staff provide the training?

3. *Who will participate?* Library media specialists, principals, and teachers need consistent training across the district so that all participants have the same knowledge base.

4. *Participation should be voluntary.* The desire to implement a flexible access program must originate from within a school rather than be imposed from outside. Teachers, administrators, and library media specialists must be convinced of the benefits and possibilities of such a program and plan jointly for it. Those who are coerced tend to find fault and convey negative feelings to the other participants. On the other hand, those who attend voluntarily are more likely to be committed to the concept of flexible access programs and to be enthusiastic supporters in their school.

5. *Make the plan flexible to allow for participants who are at different levels or stages of implementation.* The district's role after the initial training of principals and teachers will become more passive as each school develops an institutionalized plan for in-service throughout the year.

In-service Topics

District in-service for principals and teachers should concentrate on how, in their respective roles, they can create the desirable climate for flexible access implementation. The principal may be trained in developing options to allow for flexible use of library media resources, facilities, and staff. The teacher may be trained in options for scheduling use of library media staff. Both types of participants should visit schools to observe a flexible access program in action.

In addition to encompassing the obvious flexible access program implementation training for library media specialists, the district plan might include sessions, such as:

- *Production of materials.* Specific learning materials production, or "Make and Take." Library media specialists could focus each session on a different topic. One session might be to create units to correlate information skills into the district science curriculum; another might be to develop orientation materials for each grade level.

- *Creating scope and sequence documents.* Adapting the district level scope and sequence of information skills to meet the needs of individual schools.

- *Selection and weeding.* How does a flexible access library media program affect selection and weeding of materials?

- *Existing curriculum.* What is taught at the second-grade level in social studies? Have the district curriculum coordinators share their areas of expertise with the library media specialists. Such workshops are excellent district-wide public relations.

- *Examining new curriculum trends.* All new programs affect the library media program. As curriculum decisions are made at the district level, introduce all new programs to the building level library media specialists.

- *Teaching strategies.* If library media specialists lack skills in effective teaching strategies, the district in-service might provide such training. A library media specialist can be an expert cataloger but ineffective in teaching students to search an online catalog.

- *Arranging facilities.* Suggestions from experience and from the literature in facilities management are good in-service topics. Several articles in the literature may help in the planning of such an in-service.[2]

- *Assisting teachers in teaching.* Turner's *Helping Teachers Teach* can provide the basis for a most successful in-service.[3] Participants could each contribute a case study to compile a district casebook patterned after Turner's casebook.[4]

TAKING INSPIRATION FROM OTHERS

It takes so much time to implement flexible access in an individual school; isn't it a monumental task to implement programs throughout a district? It is. However, districts throughout the nation are managing successfully the implementation of flexible access programs. The interviews conducted in preparation for this book revealed a number of models worthy of emulation. The experiences of these successful persons provide clues not only to their program contents, but also to their methods of implementation.

As a district director, Judy Carnal had decided that although she had had a flexibly scheduled program for six years in her previous position, it would be difficult to implement flexible scheduling in all nine of the existing schools and the construction of a planned new school might provide the perfect opportunity to initiate such a program. In the end, financial problems provided the impetus to implementation of flexible access programs in her district:

> The opportunity to implement flexible scheduling came in a rather peculiar way. The district needed to make reductions in staff to avoid a large budget deficit. After the decision was made to cut the full-time library aides from all nine elementary schools, I was able to work with the assistant superintendent for elementary education to prepare a presentation for elementary principals. This meeting came immediately after the Board of Education voted to cut the library aides. I talked with them about the information age and the different demands today's students will face during their careers. I told them that if we tried to maintain our programs with the current rigid schedules designed for a library media specialist and aide with just the professional, we would begin to backslide or at best just maintain our current program. I suggested that the current program, though well prepared and delivered, was inadequate for the increased demands of the information age. Then I began to present the case for flexible scheduling. I explained what a fully flexible program would be like. I used a card catalog lesson as an example, explaining how it would be presented in a rigid program and how that would differ in a flexible,

integrated program. Emphasis was given to compacting the lessons and to the benefits of tying the skill to a curricular need. Then I gave them several alternate steps between a full rigid schedule and a flexible schedule. I asked them to meet with their library media specialists to determine what would work best for them. I reminded them that no two schools are the same and that they might want to consider any one of the alternatives. I did ask that they plan on at least reducing rigid classes to a maximum length of 30 minutes so that there would be time for some flexible activities. Beyond that, I left it up to them. I anticipated that I might have two or three schools choose to make the change.

Two weeks later, I brought in a media director and library media specialist from a neighboring district that had implemented flexible scheduling in two schools one semester before. They talked to the principals and library media specialists together and then just to library media specialists. That session was very helpful. Somehow it helps to hear the message from an outside authority.

A one hour meeting was held with library media specialists and principals just before the start of school to discuss how to present this program to the staff. At this point eight schools were ready to participate. (The ninth school began in October.) We brainstormed what we viewed as positives and negatives and then discussed how we might help teachers see the positives. This was extremely helpful.

In almost every building, library media specialist and principal met with small groups of teachers to present their expectations for the program.[5]

At the beginning of this chapter, Carolyn Cain described a vision of district level support for the library media program. A document created for her schools, *Flexible Scheduling in Library Media Programs: An Information Paper*, argues for school retention of the option for flexibly accessed library media programs:

Madison schools range widely in size. While smaller schools may have enough open time, even with some scheduled classes, to support classroom learning activities and project work, larger schools find their entire day taken up with scheduled classes, and the role of the LMC in supporting classroom curriculum is severely limited.

When library media specialists are scheduled as teachers of library skills classes unrelated to classroom assignments, they must spend considerable time planning for these classes. This is time that could better be spent cooperatively planning library center activities with classroom teachers and on developing the collection so that appropriate learning resources are readily available.

As our schools identify more and more students who need individualized help or specially adapted programs, the library media center is the logical place to facilitate this kind of learning opportunity. At risk students and others with special learning needs require personalized attention from the library media specialist and access to the library media center with its variety of resources. Heavily scheduled classes in the LMC preclude either resources or staff being readily available for helping such students.

Many of our library media centers are rooms with no walls and which are designed for easy and continual access into the center by students and small groups. Conducting regular classes in these settings is difficult and makes it impossible for the center to function as it was intended.

Library media specialists cannot deliver a complete LMC program if they are tied to the library media center for extended periods with classes. The demands of modern audiovisual equipment and new instructional resources such as computers often require that the library media specialist leave the center and assist the teacher in the classroom. The ability of the library media specialist to assist with special events such as accompanying a class on a field trip is also limited if regular classes are scheduled each day.

In heavily scheduled programs it is difficult for the library media specialist to do any planning with teachers. When the teacher has planning time the library media specialist is not available since he/she is working with the teacher's class, or is busy with some other scheduled class. Without the ready availability of the library media specialist inherent in flexibly scheduled programs, teachers and library media specialists have little opportunity to develop the kind of planning partnerships needed for full integration of the media program into classroom instruction.

Library media specialists should not be considered special teachers with a separate curriculum to teach. Instead, they should be viewed as the resource specialist who can help the classroom teacher select appropriate instructional materials for the students, and as a partner with each teacher in helping students develop information access skills and a love of reading and learning.[6]

Carol Kearney, director of school libraries Department of Education, Buffalo, New York, explains their program as follows:

In 1973 when I became the director, I was committed to flexible scheduling. There was research available to point to, which indicated that retention was greater when students learned when they had a need rather than on a prescribed schedule. I had already successfully conducted such a program which teachers subscribed to, and as part of my interview I made it very clear that flexible scheduled library programming was my goal. I was also very grateful to find there were a few people on staff who were ready. I do not mean to indicate that over the years there were not and do not continue to be those administrators, teachers and library media specialists who much prefer a regularly scheduled program. However, I continue to work with administrators and library media specialists, share the research, communicate the advantage of flexible scheduling, and provide appropriate staff development for the library media specialist.[7]

She offers the following advice to directors who want to move from rigid scheduling to a flexible program:

- Help library media specialists to see themselves as leaders. They must feel capable of creating change; that they are change agents; that they have something that is so important to the instruction of students that teachers will be excited about working with the library media specialist. They must not feel the teacher is too busy and they don't want to bother with them. An extensive staff development program on leadership skills is imperative.

- Provide staff development program for library media specialists on management of flexibly scheduled programs including the research, successful programs, and possible pitfalls. Library media specialists must be committed to the concept or it will not be successful. I can point to schools in our district that are very structured but because of the library media specialist, have a wonderful flexibly scheduled program.

- Work with a few library media specialists, initially, to help them develop a program and then move on to other schools.

- Provide staff development for teachers so they understand the value of flexible scheduling and resource-based teaching. Teachers will understand that this is not just an idea of one librarian.

- Provide continual interference (if this is needed) and support for the library media specialist.[8]

Carol Kearney concludes her suggestions with, "I cannot overemphasize that it is the commitment of the individual library media specialist that makes the program successful and without that he/she will find many reasons to eliminate the concept from the library media center in quick order."[9]

The pilot concept Carol Kearney suggests has been implemented successfully in Brevard County, Florida. Maureen Dugan, media resource teacher, describes that experience in an article originally published in *Florida Media Quarterly* and reprinted here. It seems a fitting conclusion to both this chapter and this book.

Flexible Scheduling, So What?*

I am a library media specialist. Prior to being a library media specialist I was a fourth grade teacher. With my Master's degree in Library/Media, I moved on to the elementary library media center for five years or so; then on to a large library media center that served both a junior high school and a high school for a three year tenure. Now I'm at the district level with responsibility for the K-12 media program for the sixty-five schools in Brevard County.

As an elementary library media specialist, I was in a school that scheduled its library media center seven periods a day, five days a week to provide the negotiated planning period for classroom teachers. As the years passed, unable to plan with teachers and schedule meaningful activities using library media center resources, I became more and more frustrated with my inability to perform as I was trained, as a professional who provided a wide variety of services to teachers and students with an important role in the education of those students. FLEXIBLE SCHEDULING! SURELY THAT WAS THE ANSWER.

At the secondary level, flexible scheduling was an established policy in the library media center. It would be possible to plan with teachers. Oh, the creative, meaningful activities that would take place using all the wonderful resources available at this well-staffed facility (four library media specialists and four clerks)! In reality, teachers were too busy; department meetings and department head meetings were few and far between if we were notified at all; the library media center sign-up sheet was full but we rarely had prior notification of what the teacher was planning to do during the time he/she had scheduled. Over the three year period, inroads were made on individual basis with several teachers, and the faculties of both schools became more aware of the professional services the library media specialists could provide and the wide spectrum of resources available in the library media center. However, it was very apparent that of and by itself, FLEXIBLE SCHEDULING WAS NOT THE ANSWER!

As Media Resource Teacher at the district level, I am excited by the opportunity to have an impact on the whole media program. For three years I have wrestled with the problem of the discrepancy between the professional responsibilities of the elementary and secondary library media specialists. It has become painfully clear that changes will not occur at the elementary level without being negotiated—a remote possibility at best—unless the school level administrators are convinced that these changes will be of enormous benefit to students and teachers alike.

---

*Reprinted with permission from Maureen S. Dugan, "Flexible Scheduling, So What?" *Florida Media Quarterly* 14 (Fall 1988): 8-10.

At the secondary level, flexible scheduling is a given but library media specialists are still encountering many obstacles in the pursuit of their goal, integration of the library media center resources into the existing curriculum. So again, support of the school level administration seems to be the key. WHAT IS THE ANSWER?!

I'm not convinced that we've found it, but in our district we made an attempt during the 1987-1988 school year to approach the problem and to find a possible solution. We instituted a pilot, CURRICULUM-INTEGRATED MEDIA SKILLS INSTRUCTION, at three schools: an elementary, a junior high school, and a senior high school. This pilot is based upon cooperative planning between library media specialist and teachers with the objective of increasing the use of the library media center and its materials by students and teachers. Evaluations by teachers, administrators, and library media specialists who participated in the pilots have indicated that they have been very successful.

The following is a detailed explanation of what has been involved in the pilot this year. It is of critical importance that the two factors indicated below be present in a school before this concept can be implemented, even as a pilot. Although numbered, these factors are equally important and both must exist for a successful implementation.

1. Absolute commitment of the library media specialist to the concept of cooperative planning with teachers. This concept is not intended to free the library media specialist to deal with the administrative responsibilities related to the smooth operation of the library media center. It does involve the library media specialist in a meaningful teaching process which integrates information skills with the existing curriculum. The library media specialist spends a great deal of time planning with teachers of all curriculum areas and grade levels and developing relevant activities to enhance and expand upon those going on in the classroom. This provides students with the opportunity to use and develop materials in many different formats and the opportunity to develop critical thinking skills in the retrieval and use of information accessed during these integrated lessons.

2. Support of the administration. At the elementary level, in order to implement this program, the library media specialist must be free to plan with teachers and schedule activities involving the library media center that may take an hour, or many hours, spread over several days. This means having a library media center with a flexible timetable and a library media specialist who is not tied into a schedule that provides planning periods for classroom teachers. Administrators of elementary schools must look for scheduling patterns that accommodate this program. At both elementary and secondary levels, classroom teachers need to know that the administration is committed to the cooperative planning concept. With this concept, as with anything new, there is the fear of the untried, and support of the administration will help avert this response. In many cases administrators will be actively involved in the planning and implementation of the activities themselves.

If involved in the pilot, the schools' administration, library media specialist(s), and I begin by working two days with a consultant who is a practicing library media specialist in a school which is involved in this program in another county. On the first day library media specialist(s), administration, and consultant meet to discuss the program and develop strategies for implementation at that particular school. Either on the afternoon of the first day or the morning of the second day, the consultant will present the program to the teachers at a faculty meeting. The second day is spent meeting with the teachers who were targeted for participation during the strategy session the previous day. During the meetings with teachers the pilot is explained and the initial preparations for the cooperative planning venture begin.

After the departure of the consultant, the participants carry out the plans that had been made during the two day sessions. I am available for support and the consultant spends one or two more days during the year to guide, make suggestions, and help evaluate the program.

A few of the many benefits to such a program follow:

1. Students are exposed to resource-based education which broadens their learning beyond the textbook.

2. Students have the opportunity to use a variety of materials in various formats, with a greater chance of finding a medium which would match their learning styles.

3. Students learn how to find, interpret, and use the information found in library media centers, skills that would have lifelong implications in an information age.

4. Students are introduced to audio-visual production as a vehicle for reporting results of their research.

5. Students are encouraged to read for personal enjoyment. As recent research indicates, the amount of independent, silent reading done by a student relates to gains in reading achievement.

6. The library media specialist becomes very familiar with the curricula, teachers and students and is able to develop a collection which is tailored to the needs of the students, teachers, and curricula of his/her school.

7. The teachers and library media specialists are able to plan activities using the library media center and its materials, incorporating information skills with the existing curriculum, thus enriching planning with the ideas of two or more minds.

8. With both teacher and library media specialist involved in the teaching process, students benefit from more individualized attention.

These are but a few of the obvious benefits of Brevard's collegial planning pilot, Curriculum-Integrated Media Skills Instruction; there are many more that are less obvious.

At a recent national teleconference which introduced *Information Power*, new national guidelines for school library media centers, Carol-Ann Haycock, former co-editor of the Canadian professional journal *Emergency Librarian*, commented that research results on schools in Canada that had such programs were just beginning to come in and that these early reports suggested that benefits to student learning could be exponential.

Information Power emphasizes the importance of the library media specialist's involvement in cooperative planning with teachers and the integration of the teaching of information skills into the existing curriculum. Dr. Philip Turner of the University of Alabama presents a model for library media specialists who wish to become involved in the instructional design process in his book, *Helping Teachers Teach*. He helps the library media specialists decide at what level they are already involved in the instructional design process and gives suggestions as to how to become more involved. More and more sessions at media conferences are concerned with this concept. Most library media specialists are aware of the trend toward integration of skills and cooperative planning. Some library media specialists will never be convinced that this is their role in the school.

Most administrators and teachers are not aware that this role for library media specialists is even a possibility. They probably have not read *Helping Teachers Teach*, probably won't read *Information Power*, and never have a session at their professional conferences on the importance of the integration of information skills into the curriculum. Some of them would probably never be convinced that this cooperative planning role for library media specialists is feasible or desirable.

I think that students currently enrolled in programs to become certified or receive a Master's degree in school library/media receive the training necessary to plan cooperatively with teachers to integrate information skills into the curriculum. They are frustrated when reality does not meet this ideal. However, administrators and teachers are not introduced to this role of the school's library media center or library media specialists in their degree programs. This is a problem that must be addressed if there is going to be a school media program that supports this concept.

The solution then, as I see it, is the education of library media specialists, teachers and administrators in the concept of cooperative planning and the integration of information skills into the curriculum. If library media specialists are ever to assume their appropriate role in the education of students this training must be incorporated into the education majors at both the undergraduate and graduate levels and must be included in district level staff development programs.

FLEXIBLE SCHEDULING IS NOT THE QUESTION OR THE ANSWER! The more accurate question/answer is the marriage of the curriculum with media resources and the acceptance of the library media specialist as a professional equal with the necessary expertise to work cooperatively with teachers and administrators to incorporate information skills using these resources. However, flexible scheduling of the library media center is a necessary element of a school program that supports this important educational concept.

In Brevard County, as a result of this year's pilot, five more elementary, three more junior high/middle, and three more high schools have expressed interest in participating in next year's continuation of the pilot. The pilot assures administrative support and provides the library media specialists, administrators, and teachers of the schools involved with training in this educational concept. Because of the number of schools that will be involved next year, different strategies will have to be developed to carry out the training of the participants. The results are worth the efforts of all those who participate.

It is our responsibility as library media specialists who are aware of the possibilities for our students to share our knowledge, increase our sphere of influence, make our presence known to those who have the power to make the necessary changes.

PROFESSIONAL ACTIVITIES

1. Prepare a prioritized list of objectives for the district to help you implement your flexible access library media program. Make an appointment to discuss your priorities with district level library media personnel.

NOTES

[1]Carolyn Cain (library media director, Madison, Wisconsin), response to questionnaire from author, 1990.

[2]Persis Emmett Rockwood and Christine Koontz Lynch, "Library Media Center Layout: A Marketing-Based Plan," in *School Library Media Annual*, edited by Shirley R. Aaron and Pat Scales (Littleton, Colo.: Libraries Unlimited, 1986), 6: 297-306; Andrew R. J. Yeaman, "Vital Signs: Cures for Confusion," *School Library Media Journal* 35 (November 1989): 23-27.

[3]Philip M. Turner, *Helping Teachers Teach: A School Library Media Specialist's Role* (Littleton, Colo.: Libraries Unlimited, 1985).

[4]Philip M. Turner, *A Casebook for "Helping Teachers Teach"* (Englewood, Colo.: Libraries Unlimited, 1988).

[5]Judy Carnal (library media director, MSD Perry Township, Indianapolis, Indiana), response to questionnaire from author, 1990.

[6]*Flexible Scheduling in Library Media Programs: An Information Paper* (Madison, Wisconsin: Public Schools, May, 1989).

[7]Carol Kearney (director of school libraries, Buffalo, New York), response to questionnaire from author, 1990.

[8]Ibid.

[9]Ibid.

ADDITIONAL READINGS

Adcock, Donald C. "The District Library Media Supervisor's Role in Promoting Information Skills. In *School Library Media Annual*, edited by Shirley L. Aaron and Pat Scales, 5: 186-87. Littleton, Colo.: Libraries Unlimited, 1987.

Kroeker, Lois Hokanson. "Behind Schedule: A Survey of West Texas Schools." *School Library Journal* 35 (December 1989): 24-28.

Toor, Ruth. "Make Your Point: (In)flexible Scheduling." *School Library Journal* (November 1987): 46.

Appendix A

Flexible Access A to Z (An Alphabet of Thoughts) *

Adventuring with media

Broadens student, parent, staff interest in the media center. It is

Correlated with every area of the curriculum.

Definite goals produce an

Enthusiastic response.

Flexible teaching time provides

Graphic results with plenty of

Hands-on application of skills. This creates

Independent media users! The

Job description no longer includes "babysitter" because

Kids are on task.

Lesson plans are written cooperatively.

Magnify the role of the media center in your school. See to it that there are

Numerous occasions for student contact. Provide

Opportunities for enrichment. Even

Physical education can be integrated! Work for

Quality, not quantity. Have students do

Research at the time of need or interest. That's when

Students benefit. Organize carefully to have

Time for all responsibilities. Be

Unscheduled but not unplanned. Be

Valuable. Make

Wise use of personnel, facilities, and materials.

Xerox this for your principal.

You can do it!

Zealous media specialists are "filled with eagerness and ardent interest in pursuit of excellence."

---

*Created by Cheryl Jessup and Jan Buchanan for the Florida Association of Media Education (FAME) Conference, 1985.

Appendix B

*The "So You Want to Be Flexible" Test**

(Circle your answers)

1. Do you enjoy being on your feet all day?   YES   NO

2. Can you smile politely at the teacher who interrupts while you are instructing students?   YES   NO

3. Can you formulate a lesson for teaching guide words in a biographical dictionary to fifth grade students on short notice?   YES   NO

4. Do you carry a paper and/or lesson plan book and pencil at all times?   YES   NO

5. Does it bring tears of joy to your eyes when students gather at the public catalog?   YES   NO

6. Are you embarrassed when most of your media collection is sitting neatly on the shelves?   YES   NO

7. Can you stay calm when a teacher plays "I Spy" in your plan book?   YES   NO

8. Are you ecstatic when students want to use filmstrips, cassettes, records, etc.?   YES   NO

9. Do you say to a questioning student "No appointment necessary" rather than "Sorry, see you Tuesday at 10:00 when Mrs. Smith's class is scheduled in the media center."?   YES   NO

10. Would you like to develop the showmanship of a ringmaster by simultaneously coordinating a class checking out, large group instruction, small group research and individual users while changing a projector lamp?   YES   NO

---

*Created by Cheryl Jessup and Jan Buchanan for the Florida Association of Media Education (FAME) Conference, 1985.

11. When the cataloging, correspondence and selection
    tools layer your desk like an archaeological dig,
    can you turn aside with a smile to assist students
    and teachers?   YES   NO

12. Would you like your principal to observe you
    teaching skills that are relevant to student needs?   YES   NO

13. Do you want to leave skidmarks in the hallway racing
    materials to a teacher who has just begun a new unit? YES   NO

If you answered mostly yeses, what are you waiting for? You possess some of the traits necessary for a flexible access program.

If you answered mostly no's, give serious consideration to whether or not a flexible access program is for you.

Appendix C

"Flexible Access and You" Script

by Terry Campanella
(Can be read orally by any number of readers)

(Numbers at left match corresponding illustrations that follow the script.)

1. For most of us, as far back in our teaching career as we can remember, the library media center has been the place we dropped off our class and began our thirty minute whirlwind race of grading, running off papers, planning, etcetera.

2. We really never knew or even cared to know what was going on in there.

3. For the library media specialist these thirty minutes represented the challenge of a lifetime. She had to collect books being returned, read or share a story with the class, teach a skill, allow the students to choose new books, check out new books, line them up, send them off and greet the next class.

4. In actuality only about 1/50 of her time was spent actually teaching.

5. Can you imagine what it would be like to teach a subject, let's say math, for less than thirty minutes once a week with no opportunity for practice, or to extend that lesson that was just beginning to go great?

6. I'd venture to say that by the end of the year the students would have mastered very few math skills. As teachers, we know that in order to teach to mastery, we must be able to review, teach, provide practice and recap at the end of each lesson.

7. We also know that students learn best when they can find some practical use for what they are learning and that most lessons (not all), call for planning.

8. With these solid principles in mind we are about to embark on a new program that will prove to be exciting and rewarding for the library media specialist, you the teacher and most importantly, our students.

A number of illustrations appear at the end of this appendix as examples of simple artwork that can be made into transparencies and used with an overhead projector to accompany this script.

9. The program I am speaking of is Flexible Access.

10. When you first hear the term you may think that it implies that the purpose of the library media center this year is just to allow students and teachers to come and go as they please with no direction or plan, but nothing could be further from the truth.

11. What flexible access does mean is that we, teachers and library media specialist, as a team will determine the use of the library media center based on the needs and interests of our students.

12. For example, for some teachers just the two little words "Science Fair" can set fear in their hearts. How do I get 25 to 30 students through picking a topic, researching it, writing it up and include how to locate bibliographic information?

13. Well, through cooperative planning with your library media specialist, you may find a list of topic suggestions that can be easily researched in the school library media center and that she would be most happy to take the students through the steps of writing a research paper.

14. Since many of the tools needed for writing such a paper are part of the Florida curriculum, the library media specialist may want to use this time to teach or reinforce other information skills.

15. The best part of this is that together you will decide the amount of time you will need to devote to this project. You may decide that meeting one hour every day for two weeks will be the best approach. With flexible access this is now possible. Let's recap:

16. 1. Skills are not taught in isolation but rather at point of need.
    2. Blocks of time are scheduled rather than a thirty minute slot once a week.
    3. Joint teaching and planning allows students to benefit from a smaller pupil/teacher ratio and also allows each professional to use their expertise.

17. How else can this schedule benefit you, the teacher, and the students? Small groups can also use the library media center. They may come to do research, complete an assignment, just to browse or as part of the enrichment activity in your three part reading plan. Why not use the library media center as a station?

18. For example, Mrs. M is having difficulty teaching sequencing to one of her reading groups. After discussing and planning with the library media specialist, it is decided that the students will come to the library media center as part of their reading wheel. There they will view filmstrips and do some hands-on sequencing with the library media specialist.

19. And what about Johnny, you know the student I am speaking about. He seems to devour books! Even though he checked out a book at the regularly scheduled class time on Tuesday, here it is Thursday and he is asking when you are going back. Flexible access will allow Johnny to come into the library media center any time during the school day. Let's recap:

20. 1. Library media center can be used as a reading center or for small group instruction.
    2. Students may check out books at any time or day of the week.
    3. Classes can still check out books at a set scheduled time.

21. Last but not least, let's look at Mrs. G's class. On a nature walk over school grounds, they spotted a black and yellow butterfly they had never seen before. Because of flexible access, their first stop when they get back into the building can be the library media center. There they look through butterfly books and discover the name of the beautiful creature they have just seen. Remember I said that most lessons are planned but not all. Flexible access allows us to make the most of those precious teachable moments.

22. Sounds great, you say. Where do we begin? Well, like every good program, we must begin with planning.

23. At the end of this tape your library media specialist will share some tools that will make planning easy.

24. The first is a way of prioritizing what aspects of the media program are most important to your grade level and students.

25. The second will be a form on which you will be asked to share your nine week overall plan for each subject area.

26. The third will be a weekly planning sheet that will be used for your cooperative planning with your library media specialist.

27. And last, you will be asked to set up a cooperative planning time with your library media specialist. This may be as often as once a week or as little as once a month.

    According to *Information Power*, the guidelines for school library media programs put out by the American Library Association, "an individual's success in the next century will depend on the ability to access, evaluate and use information." With flexible access, together we can provide the keys to success.

    With flexible access we are all winners, teachers, library media specialists and most of all students.

Flexible Access

9 | 10

11 | 12

17

18

19

1. Media center can be used as a reading center or for small group instruction

2. Students may check out books at any time or day of the week

3. Classes can still check out books at a set scheduled time

20

21

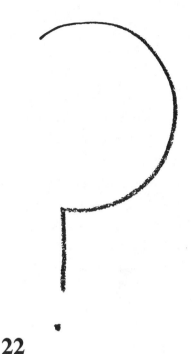

22

Tools needed for Planning

23

Things to consider when Prioritizing:

1. Age and grade level you teach
2. What motivates your students
3. Learning style of students
4. Interests of your students
5. Your interests
6. What you have found successful before
7. Special students needs
8. What sounds appealing

24

Things to consider for Over all plan

1. Be sure to include each subject area
2. Plan should be general ex. we will be studying plants
3. Give a time frame ex 3 weeks or May 3-June 3
4. Be sure to include any special projects you have planned ex. we plan to start a vegetable garden
5. Include any plans that may involve the media specialist ex. would like weekly video of garden

25

Things to consider for Weekly planning

1. Follow guidelines for Over all planning but make these plans more specific ex. students will learn parts of plants
2. Pinpoint any area in which additional resources may be needed ex. we would like some simple experiments that can be done with plants.
3. List any resources you know you want to use ex. model of flower

26

Teachers
Media Specialist
most
of all
Students

27

Appendix D

*Through the Eyes of a Teacher**

Carolyn Durak
Fifth Grade Teacher
Wilson Elementary School
Sanford, Florida

At first I was wary. After all, it is *more* plan time elementary teachers need — not *less*! We had been informed that this new "Open Media" approach could only work if the new media specialist were not tied down with weekly full-sized classes. Translation: no thirty-minute bonus plan slot! Our principal had already made his request for us to be "supportive" and "flexible." Translation: we were not allowed to complain. Nevertheless, I had taught long enough to know that what looks good on paper was often unrecognizable in operation. This was not my first time to hear of this "Open Media" concept. My principal had encouraged two of us to observe in another school the previous year. I had come back guardedly enthusiastic about a media program, TIC TOC (Totally Integrated Curriculum Through Open [Media] Center), which theoretically allowed students to come in small groups as an extension of the classroom — and the media specialist would supervise their research needs, teach reference skills, or provide learning centers to support the classroom!

The lead teacher in fifth grade was currently scheduling each of her reading groups in the media center one day each week as part of her "wheel" of reading instruction. I was amazed that such appointments were actually available *during* her class's reading time! My scrutiny was met with assurance that, while no classes could *ever* be "sent" wholesale to media except when accompanied by the classroom teacher, *every* class might expect to be scheduled any week through cross-planning between the media specialist and the teacher. Furthermore, each single teacher might schedule groups in any given week, which might cycle each student through a period of instruction — in addition to book circulation privileges or independent research access at other times. This program definitely had my interest.

And now it was to be part of *my* school. Well, my principal had a good track record for hiring decisions. He also was no sucker for empty educational fads. I knew there was a better than average chance that our school could profit by the implementation of this program. We were obviously going to give it a try.

The first score went to TIC TOC — it became immediately clear that the concept of a totally integrated media curriculum was inseparable from the concept that media centers are there for students and teachers to use. I had seen enough media specialists "guard" the books from the children! A second score

---

*Reprinted with permission from Carolyn Durak, "Through the Eyes of a Teacher," *Florida Media Quarterly* 14 (Fall 1988): 19, 22.

was made when I realized the potential for allowing children to check out books spontaneously or in small groups while I helped others finish a task in my classroom! I had always disliked the mass classwide book-check—too much time wasted waiting on each other and a poor atmosphere to provide for interested browsing of books.

Points were lost when I realized that time needed to be devoted to cross-planning with this media specialist every week; otherwise, this was a resource that would go untapped. Also, automatic slots for my children in the media center did not exist. I could never again leave my class with the media specialist and go off by myself to prepare a lesson; always, I was expected to remain with my students if the entire class were in the media center.

However, when one of my fifth graders, Dick, took me on for his sixth-round argument challenging my thesis that it is illogical to classify Eurasia as two continents, I could allow him to explore his theory that, perhaps, they were each geologically part of separate continental plates. When Christy's starfish research came up missing several key pieces of information during our editing conference, she could head straight for the media center without having to wait to see if our media specialist had a class. When Brian heard that his original piece of fiction resembled *My Side of the Mountain*, he could spontaneously pursue his curiosity in time to have the book in his hands before the day's sustained silent reading. Fifty-five students, one-by-one, funneled through our media center to use the opaque projector in tracing an outline for their illustrations to publish their finished "Founding Father Biopoems."

Slowly I began to believe that the benefits of this totally integrated curriculum concept could be well worth whatever sacrifices we might be making. In trade for my once-a-week appointment was the flexibility that could meet my needs for remediation skill groups four days in a row!

As a specialist in integrated curriculum, our media specialist can respond to classroom needs in ways which can more than replace that thirty-minute "plan" slot once afforded through "library class" once each week. When my team-teaching colleague discovered a weakness in our fifth graders' performance on the SSAT, he conferred with our media specialist; she designed and led a relay activity in determining appropriate reference sources. Likewise, as my colleague requested assistance in strengthening a reading skill, our media specialist led a hands-on newspaper activity for his classes. When my students were beginning a source search for research on an Indian project, they were taught by the media specialist a format for recording their bibliography—with "rights-for-conference" granted individually in the weeks to come to proofread each effort. As we approached writing our own fictional or autobiographical "Holiday Treasure" stories, our media specialist shared examples from literature of "beginnings" other writers have used. She provided an introduction to folktales in preparation for a marionette performance of the Pied Piper. She is presently preparing centers to extend vocabulary and concepts needed for awareness of solids and masses in math and science.

Perhaps the key to the success of this media program is that our children are taught independent use of its resources from kindergarten up. Only now am I beginning to take for granted the sight of a five-year-old returning a book to the media center — confidently, and alone; browsing the shelves for a new one; checking out her new choice by herself; and perhaps leaving the media center having never once sought the attention of an adult in the period of ten minutes. This degree of independence means that, as in a public library, students need not be denied use of library resources just because the media specialist "has a class."

I was honored to be asked to represent the teacher's viewpoint for TIC TOC. Our school is now halfway through our second year with a flexible access program, and exciting things are happening. I guess you can tell — I've decided I can't do without it. I'm not sure any elementary school should.

Appendix E
Publishers

The Horn Book, Inc.
31 St. James Ave.
Boston, MA 02116
   The Horn Book publication's regular feature, "Books in the Classroom," provides specific suggestions for using children's books.

Libraries Unlimited/Teacher Ideas Press
P.O. Box 3988
Englewood, CO 80155-3988
   School Library Media File: Folders of Ideas for Library Excellence, an annual publication, provides instructional activities and creative programs submitted by practicing media specialists.

LMS Associates
17 East Henrietta St.
Baltimore, MD 21230
   The "Into the Curriculum" column of *School Library Media Activities Monthly* includes fully developed activities in lesson plan format solicited from the readership. "Activity Almanac" provides descriptions of activities related to holidays, historical events, birthdays, and other significant days of each month.

The Ohio State University
Room 200, Ramseyer Hall
29 West Woodruff
Columbus, OH 43210
   The WEB (Wonderfully Exciting Books) is a quarterly publication devoted to reviewing children's books and suggesting ways to use them in the classroom. Each issue has an extensive web of possibilities for a particular subject or unit.

The Perfection Form Company
1000 North Second Ave.
Logan, IA 51546

Each teacher's guide in the Reading Beyond the Basal series focuses on a single title of quality children's literature. Each book presents critical thinking, oral language, and cross-curriculum activities. The Reading Beyond the Basal Plus guides offer a broad range of activities for individual titles appropriate for intermediate students. Celebrate Literature is a comprehensive literature activity guide series for kindergarten through fifth grade. A separate guide introduces genre and elements appropriate for that particular grade. These guides make a perfect core for a literature-based flexible access library media program.

Pied Piper Productions
P.O. Box 320
Verdugo City, CA 91046

The Literature for Children series introduces information skills through quality children's literature. The filmstrips for intermediate students focus on literary genre and the primary filmstrips on particular subjects.

Allen Raymond, Inc.
11 Hall Lane
Box 1266
Darien, CT 06820

A double-spread calendar, "Teaching Day by Day," is included in each issue of *Early Years*. Suggested daily activities center around a common theme.

Appendix F

Introducing Information Skills with Literature

Anno, Mitsumasa. *Anno's U.S.A.* New York: Philomel, 1983.
Each of the illustrations in this wordless picture book provides a multitude of topics for research.

"Atlas." *Compton's Precyclopedia*, vol. 1. Chicago: F. E. Compton Co., 1977.
A perfect introduction for an initial atlas lesson for third graders.

Batherman, Muriel. *Some Things You Should Know about My Dog*. Englewood Cliffs, N.J.: Prentice Hall, 1976.
Fourth graders enjoy using the thesaurus to rewrite the story for kindergarteners. Appropriate substitutes are found for the adjectives describing the dog.

Bayer, Jane. *A, My Name Is Alice*. New York: Dial, 1984.
Primary student alphabetizing skills are reinforced by writing a book patterned after this one. Intermediate students research the unusual animals and locate the exotic places.

Dahl, Roald. *The Magic Finger*. New York: Harper, 1966.
Read the first chapter. Use the overhead projector to view the illustration of the teacher. Demonstrate the uses and operation of the projector. Students can create similar illustrations to share with the class.

Feeling, Muriel. *Moja Means One: Swahili Counting Book*. New York: Dial, 1971.
After sharing this title, introduce special dictionaries. Students then use foreign language dictionaries to create their own book patterned after this one.

Lobel, Arnold. *Mouse Soup*. New York: Harper, 1977.
After enjoying activities using the table of contents, prepare some delicious mouse soup.

Sobol, Donald J. *Encyclopedia Brown Takes the Case*. Nashville, Tenn.: Thomas Nelson, 1973.
Any of the Encyclopedia Brown titles provide the perfect introduction for an initial encyclopedia lesson.

Wyler, Rose, and Gerald Ames. *Prove It!* New York: Harper Row, 1963.
All students remember the arrangement of the 500's when introduced with "Chase the Pepper" on the overhead projector.

Appendix G

A Simple Manual Circulation System

The author's manual circulation system answers the question we most frequently have to answer: "This child is withdrawing from school. Does he have any library books out?" With this system the largest number of books unaccounted for at inventory time was thirty. This simple system works as described below.

Affix a narrow label with each student's name, grade, and teacher on a tall book pocket. These labels may be supplied by your district data processing department or by your school.

Affix another name label to a number of colored book cards for each student. The use of a green card and referring to it as the student's "go" card reinforces that they are able to leave the media center after exchanging cards. The number of green cards in each student's pocket is determined by the number of items that may be circulated at any given time (certainly no fewer than twenty items).

Once assembled, these pockets are filed alphabetically by grade and/or teacher and kept at the checkout desk. Plastic ice cube bins hold approximately three hundred pockets. Adhesive numerals indicating the grade make locating the appropriate bin easy for the youngest children.

To check out a book, the child:

1. Locates his student pocket.

2. Removes a colored card from his pocket.

3. Puts the colored name card in the item pocket and the book card in his student pocket.

4. Repeats the process if taking out multiple items.

5. Reverses the procedure to return an item.

This manual system can be adapted for independent circulation with an automated circulation system. Students have one card with their patron bar code numbers filed in the same manner. Rather than use green "go" cards, red "stop" cards are used to remind students to stop to refile their bar codes before leaving the media center.

Appendix H

List of Contributors

Nell Brown
P.O. Box 353010
Palm Coast, FL 32035

Judy Carnal
MSD Perry Township
5401 S. Shelby St.
Indianapolis, IN 46227

Beverley Fonnesbeck
3771 Mattei's Road
Santa Ynez, CA 93460

Jo Ann Gadicke
1238 Geele Ave.
Cheboygan, WI 53083

Carol Hartsoe
1771 Robin's Nest Ct.
Richmond, VA 23233

Susan Heath
1916 24th Ave. W.
Palmetto, FL 34221

Curtis Jensen
2221 Greenwood Ave.
Cedar Falls, IA 50613

Carol Kearney
Director of Libraries
Buffalo Dept. of Education
418 City Hall
Buffalo, NY 14202

Kathy Kren
97 Greenfield St.
Buffalo, NY 14214

Lois Kurtman
Waterford School
95 Fourth Street
Buffalo, NY 14202

Marlene Lazzara
Henking School
2941 Linneman
Glenview, IL 60025

Shirley Ledford
Pinkhill School
P.O. Box 128
Pinkhill, NC 28572

Jane MacDonald
Ferndale School District
Grant School Library
21131 Garden Lane
Ferndale, MI 48220

Ketti Miller
Cahaba Heights School
4401 Dolly Ridge Rd.
Birmingham, Alabama 35243

Helen Rosenberg
186 Spackenkill Rd.
Poughkeepsie, NY 12603

Connie Ryle
Hillcrest Elementary School
10335 Croke Drive
Denver, CO 80221

Jean Scheu
Pilgrim Lane Elementary Media
    Center
3725 Pilgrim Lane N.
Plymouth, MN 55441

Deanne Sheppard
Lorraine Academy
71 Lorraine Ave.
Buffalo, NY 14220

Barb Stein
Roosevelt School
611 Greenwood Drive
Iowa City, IA 52246

Index